Till Death Do Us Part

Till Death Do Us Part

Love, Marriage, and the Mind of the Killer Spouse

Dr. Robi Ludwig
and Matt Birkbeck

Introduction by Larry King
Foreword by Nancy Grace

ATRIA BOOKS
New York London Toronto Sydney

1230 Avenue of the Americas
New York, NY 10020

Photographs appearing in the insert are courtesy of The Associated Press.

The Library of Congress has cataloged the hardcover edition as follows:
Till death do us part : love, marriage, and the mind of the killer spouse / Robi Ludwig and Matt Birkbeck ; introduction by Larry King; foreword by Nancy Grace.—1st Atria Books hardcover ed.
p.cm.
Includes index.
1. Uxoricide—United States—Case studies. 2. Mariticide—United States—Case studies. 3. Murderers—United States—Psychology. 4. Criminal psychology. I. Birkbeck, Matt. II. Title.

HV6542.L83 2006
364.152'3—dc22

2006040660

ISBN-13: 978-0-7432-7508-8
ISBN-10: 0-7432-7508-X
ISBN-13: 978-0-7432-7509-5 (Pbk)
ISBN-10: 0-7432-7509-8 (Pbk)

First Atria Books trade paperback edition February 2007

10 9 8 7 6 5 4 3 2 1

Manufactured in the United States of America

Dedication

To my husband David Ludwig, who has embraced my dream like it was his own, which has helped me to become who I want and need to be.

and

To my parents Helene and Charles Shalotsky, who continue to model for me what a lifelong, loving, and successful marriage is and should be.

Contents

Introduction

FRIENDS, we at *Larry King Live* follow and report on a wide variety of topics, from breaking world news to celebrity interviews. The murder of a spouse is among the topics that has always attracted intense viewer interest.

You'll recall that America, and the world, was transfixed with a very prominent spousal murder case involving Scott and Laci Peterson, and we followed that case, and others, on my program from the very beginning.

It's these kinds of cases, where there are allegations or evidence that one spouse unexpectedly turns violent toward another, that strikes at the hearts of viewers. With each new case we are mystified, frightened, compelled, and intrigued. Perhaps it's because we are taught that family is supposed to be the rock of our foundation. Family is supposed to offer us comfort and security. But when that offer is rescinded, we want to know what went amiss.

Why, we ask, in cases like Peterson, would a husband (or wife) kill his (or her) spouse? What were the signs? Could it have been prevented? What went wrong?

To answer those questions I've often turned to Dr. Robi Ludwig.

Dr. Ludwig is a psychotherapist and former reporter who has given millions of viewers an inside peek into the mind of the killer spouse, providing us with keen commentary and analysis. Through Robi's valuable insight, she has helped us all to understand the violent actions and dark logic behind these murders, particularly since many of these cases appear to involve seemingly normal people.

In these pages Dr. Robi Ludwig goes even deeper into the psyche of the killer spouse, taking real-life cases and further expanding and explaining the motivations behind each murder, helping us understand why someone would commit this kind of crime.

—*Larry King*

Foreword

FOR years I have known Dr. Robi Ludwig. Not only have I known her, I have disagreed with, argued with, listened to, and most important, learned from her. Her unique perspective, grounded in the principles of psychotherapy and the study of human behavior, has brought a new meaning to the analysis of trials and the behavior, motives, and testimony of witnesses, victims, and defendants alike. A trial lawyer's duty is to learn the facts and law of a case; a prosecutor's duty is to seek a verdict that speaks the truth; and a defense lawyer's duty is to obtain an acquittal for the client on trial. Dr. Robi Ludwig explains the "why" behind each of these.

While the state is not required to show a motive in order to prove its case, juries often search for this missing piece of reasoning. Dr. Robi not only studies the human mind and behavior, but breaks it down in terms of actual cases; cases that engage us, challenge us, make us angry, and make us cry. Yes, a jury can convict, a judge can sentence. But what good are verdicts if we fail to learn from them? This is the greatest of many reasons that I have highlighted Dr. Ludwig's in-depth and intuitive analysis on Court TV as well as CNN over and over throughout the years. She casts light on the formerly taboo subjects of marital strife and homicide.

In the Scott Peterson case, Dr. Robi Ludwig analyzed, I believe correctly, the motivations of Peterson himself, as well as various police officers, neighbors, attorneys, and family members. Who could ever forget the bombshell testimony, tapes, and court appearance on the witness stand of Peterson's lover, Amber Frey? The angry Lee and Jackie Peterson, blind to the evidence before them? The suffering of Sharon Rocha? The charming guile of Scott Peterson? And the reasoning behind the jury verdict? Dr. Ludwig accurately weighed in on each, clarifying what we observed in the courtroom.

I remember distinctly the night Robi and I sat quietly in a darkened studio, guests together on a *Larry King Live* broadcast. We were discussing the Peterson trial after hearing that homicide was the leading cause of death among pregnant women. The number-one cause of death? I couldn't believe my own ears! After all the domestic homicides and domestic assaults I had prosecuted, I was unaware of that astounding and heartbreaking statistic. In the weeks following, Dr. Ludwig began to make sense of this shocking statistic that plagues our nation.

But long before the Peterson case, Dr. Robi Ludwig was speaking out regarding marriage and murder. From Rabbi Fred Neulander, on trial for arranging the murder of his longtime wife Carol, to the murder trials of Dr. Richard Sharpe and novelist Michael Peterson, Dr. Ludwig has become the authority on marital homicide, its causes, its far-reaching implications, and the devastating wake of pain it causes.

The depth and insight she brings to the table has broadened my understanding of these heinous acts, and of the underlying darkness that is often inherent in so many marriages. Dr. Robi enlightens us all.

—*Nancy Grace*

Prologue

EACH day six people are murdered in the U.S. by a spouse or "intimate partner." Another twenty-seven hundred people daily, or almost a million per year, are physically assaulted, victims of what the U.S. Department of Justice calls "intimate-partner violence"—violent crimes such as assault, rape, and robbery perpetrated by spouses, boyfriends, and girlfriends.

Over the years many of these cases have attracted national notoriety through extensive coverage on CNN, FOX, MSNBC, Court TV, daytime and cable talk shows, the Internet, and newspapers as millions of viewers and readers try to understand why one spouse would kill another.

From David and Clara Harris to Scott and Laci Peterson to O. J. and Nicole Simpson, Americans are fascinated by behind-the-scenes stories of spousal violence. And with each new case and the continual media coverage and fascination it draws (the Peterson case was an international phenomenon while the Harris case, in which she repeatedly ran over her husband with her car, was also reported around the world, and spawned twenty-four-hour coverage, several magazine articles, a book, and even a CBS-TV movie, *Suburban Madness*), we become immersed in another form of reality TV—where the average citizen is taken deep inside the personal lives of husbands and wives to see first-hand what's gone terribly wrong in real time, from tragic event to trial.

Why the intense interest?

Perhaps because most of us, whether we admit it or not, sometimes have violent, even homicidal thoughts toward our spouse or intimate partner. While the majority never act on those thoughts, others do, and we are fascinated with these crimes and want to understand how seemingly normal, and in many cases flourishing, lives could unravel in such devastating ways. On another level, violence is a dark contrast to what so many of us still believe in—love, and the ideals and promise that marriage affords us.

Like many people, I consider myself an incurable romantic, and there is a part of me that will always believe in walking off into the sunset to live happily ever after. When I was younger, like many children, I assumed I would get married, live in a nice house, and have a couple of kids. I also assumed this very traditional achievement would bring me endless happiness and romance. So much so, that during my college years I considered girls engaged by graduation to be the epitome of success. Perhaps needless to say, I was not one of those girls.

I remained single through my twenties, and the thought of being single in my forties scared me. I simply couldn't imagine how anyone that age could live a happy life if she had yet to find her Prince Charming. To me, a woman in that situation seemed so . . . alone, and I equated marriage with all that was good and passionate in life. Of course, I knew that not all marriages were healthy or fulfilling, but I did believe that if one chose properly, her romantic ideal was just a careful selection away.

I eventually found my "romantic ideal" in David, a successful New York physician. We have two beautiful children and my husband and I have busy, hectic, and fulfilling professional and personal schedules. But during our time together my image of marriage has become more realistic: Marriage is not perpetual bliss. It's a work in progress. But knowing that hasn't changed the high priority I place on achieving a successful marital relationship for myself, as well as for my patients.

One of my specialties as a New York–based psychotherapist is creating healthy relationships. During my professional career I have found human interactions one of the most interesting and challenging aspects of my practice. One of my goals is to help my patients understand and support human connections and the contributions they make to a fulfilled and joyful life.

While my career as a therapist focuses primarily on the unifying aspects of relationships, I have become, in recent years, an expert on the deadly relationships, expanding my early career as a television reporter to discussing these cases, and the motivations behind them, before millions of television viewers who often wonder and ask the most obvious question: Why do these cases make their way into the public consciousness and permanently reside there?

It's not just due to voyeurism or an attraction to true crime. The root of the interest in these cases becomes apparent when one listens to the types of questions asked by the many callers who phone in, seeking answers.

"Robi, how could such a normal-seeming guy be driven to kill his pregnant wife?"

"Robi, why would a man drug his own girlfriend?"

"Robi, why would a woman run over her husband with a car?"

Real people want to understand the motivations that drive real people over the edge. Despite our fascination with the extravagance of celebrity lives, viewers may never be able to relate to them, but they can relate to the next-door neighbor whose seemingly stable marriage serves as a cover for violent impulses that explode in murderous assault.

I, for one, was always fascinated by the people who actually crossed over the line and acted on their most severe and devastating impulses and fantasies, in part because I was aware of my own vengeful fantasies when I was angry (without ever acting on them, of course). I was curious about why someone *would* act on such an impulse as opposed to not act on it. What made such a person different from most people?

My interest in those dark impulses widened, and today, between my television work and private practice, I deal with the very real problems of people who, in many instances, revealed their darker impulses, from engaging in affairs to committing violence. In fact, many of the marital homicide cases I've analyzed for Court TV, *Larry King Live, Nancy Grace,* and *Oprah* repeated a distinctive pattern. For example, it was not uncommon for these couples to appear to be happy and in love. Very often the cases involved "love at first sight" couples who fell head over heels for each other. Many were high school or college sweethearts and the envy of their friends and relatives. These spouses were often considered a romantic pair, beloved by their in-laws and respected within the community. No one would ever have imagined that death was right around the corner. They seemed to be too perfect and in love for that.

So again, we get back to the questions people ask me so often: How could these seemingly happy, loving couples end up killing the other? Were there any signs? Was it true that some intimate-partner homicides were more predictable than others?

The answers are both simple and complex. In some of these

marriages there was clear evidence of domestic violence that had escalated to a predictably lethal degree. In other instances the husband or wife just seemed to snap with no warning, no signs. One day they were both alive, and the next day one spouse was dead, killed by the other.

The research and discussion of these cases over the last few years captivated me as much as the audience, and I developed an expertise in understanding the motivations for this phenomenon. So when my literary agent called to ask if I might be interested in writing about marriage and murder, I was intrigued. It also struck me as ironic that I, a therapist who during the day focuses primarily on the unifying aspects of relationships, was now considering writing a book on deadly ones, the very cases I analyzed on television.

In the end, it made perfect sense. Marital homicides raised some powerful questions that needed to be explored and answered in new ways. After some research, I realized that a book examining this specific issue had much merit. Clearly there is a dark side to all relationships, though this side does not typically result in murder. Why is it, then, that some people kill while others have affairs, get divorced, or engage in more benign behaviors like complaining about their spouse?

Sigmund Freud took a slightly dim view of intimate relationships. He thought it was impossible to have a bond that lasted for any length of time without there being some residue of hostility and dislike. For most people involved in relationships, who initially tend to idealize their partner, these negative feelings become repressed, and the repression helps them feel less angry with their partners.

Culturally, we are taught that the romantic ideal is reality, and the quest for romantic perfection is a powerful drive. In some cases this quest can blind us and leave us vulnerable. When loving couples find one another and decide to unite, there is the hope that each partner will finally be cared for and valued. The last thought people have is that they are marrying a hurtful stranger. But the truth is we all marry people who on some level are unknown to us, and part of what intrigues us about couples who express their violent feelings is that they are more like us than not. But how much like us are they? So much of what has been written about intimate-partner homicide does not fully explain why these people do what they do.

Ultimately there are multiple reasons for these crimes and thus, here we are, exploring the question, could anyone marry his or her killer? Who are these men and women who turn on each other in the most deadly way, and can anyone be a victim or a perpetrator?

I have determined that there are ten specific motivations and triggers behind such murders, and this book will crystallize the profile of individuals who kill their spouses and address these relationships and the fatal moment of the crime, replaying it in slow motion so that the motive, the mind-set, and the red flags of such relationships can be illuminated. You will understand that the reasons cannot, in most cases, be reduced to the simplistic motives of control and greed. No, many of the issues are far more complex.

You may be surprised to find that these spousal killers may not be so different from the intimates in your own life, and that your spouse or intimate partner may exhibit some of the traits evident in those who kill. That's scary but surely worth knowing and understanding. After all, when loving couples exchange their vows and say "till death do us part," it's not supposed to mean "or until I get angry and decide to kill you."

1

Why Marry?

MARRIAGE is a dynamic and ever changing institution with its share of potentially major problems. Although many couples find it extremely fulfilling, just as many, if not more, find it difficult and heartbreaking.

The stark reality is that the majority of marriages fail. And many marriages are full of violence and abuse, which sometimes escalates to murder. In light of these potential drawbacks, one can raise a very good question: Why marry at all? In fact, why do human beings pair off knowing there's a greater chance the emotional and financial investment will be for naught? One could ask the question, "What's the point?"

Marriage emerged some forty-five hundred years ago and evolved into a widespread and accepted institution that bonded families, maintained order, and created wealth. Unlike today, where many of us are searching for our romantic "soul mate," marriage was originally more about economics than deep emotion. In her book *Marriage: A History,* Professor Stephanie Coontz writes that until recently marriage was considered far too important to be determined by something as irrational as love and was more or less a business venture, an institution that provided for the necessities of day-to-day existence and survival of the species. It was only over the last century that the primary motivation to marry was based on feelings and emotion rather than the ability to provide stability.

Today, given the stark reality that marriage is prone to failure, are there psychological and biological underpinnings that pull us in this direction, and not only once or twice but over and over and over again?

According to Professor David Buss, an evolutionary psychologist from the University of Texas, we as humans are designed to fall in love. However, we may not be equally as inclined to stay in love. Buss and others believe that it is "natural" for both men and women to become disenchanted with a mate, suddenly finding him/her irritating, unattractive, or totally unreasonable, their flaws revealing their true selves and the mind going into "the grass is greener" mode. For married adults this often leads to adultery.

One look at the numbers and it's easy to see that many people find their mates unsatisfactory on many levels. According to several studies, a whopping 80 percent of married males and 50 percent of married females have sex with outside partners. It's also natural for many married individuals to find some other person superior on most counts when compared to the terribly flawed spouse one is saddled with. Although this may sound hopeless in terms of achieving a successful relationship, what is natural is not necessarily unchangeable. On the flip side, long-lasting, happily married couples do feel better about their lives, and they live longer, too.

According to biological logic, men tend to look for women with physical characteristics that indicate they are at the peak of their childbearing years, while women seek security. But some believe the so-called logic of this theory is flawed.

All of us are evolutionary survivors. We had to be made of strong stock in order to survive the environmental challenges thrown our way. While both sexes are certainly vulnerable to infidelity, men are much more inclined to actually acquire additional mates (like a harem) or to engage in a casual fling.

If we look at the DNA of love, genes don't speak per se, but they do affect our behavior by creating feelings and emotions that build and are maintained, thereby altering our brain chemistry. Anthropologists have discovered what laypeople have known for years—that love between a man and woman is universal. Marriage, like love, is also universal. So marriage, at least from an evolutionary perspective, functions as a social reproductive arrangement that customarily involves the extended family and provides a way to raise a stable and healthy family.

Helen Fisher's essay "The Nature and Evolution of Romantic Love" concludes that all of these qualities—love, attraction, sexual chemistry—result in raising a family with children and increasing the chances for survival. So, to love a child and develop the appropriate paternal investment requires having certain relationships in place. From the biological perspective, the first step toward becoming loving and devoted parents was for a man and woman to develop a mutual attraction. The genetic payoff of having two parents committed to a child's welfare seems to be the main reason why men and women fall in love and swoon over one another.

Having two parents rather than one ensures a better chance for the offspring to survive and procreate. Unlike our nearest animal relatives, humans are a species of "high parental investment." In every known hunter-gatherer society, marriage is the standard—not necessarily monogamous marriage, and not always lasting marriage, but nonetheless a marriage of some sort.

WHILE marriages in the past were more practical unions than they are today (when marriage is supposed to be loved-based) people have been selecting mates since the beginning of time. And when we look for a person to spend the rest of our lives with we often imagine an ideal Mr. or Ms. Right. An ideal life partner is someone whose personality, compatibilities, and purposes align with our own. If someone corresponds to our internal image of the "perfect" dream lover, we may "fall in love" with him or her. But the fact is we can easily get turned on by men or women whom we would not and should not consider an appropriate marital partner.

So, if we decide we are going to spend most of our adult lives married to one person, we have probably built up some specific ideas about what kind of man or woman this person should be. The ideal mate for most of us would be someone who turns us on sexually, who would be a great parent, and who we can feel romantic toward. The more discerning person may select someone who he or she can live with even if their romantic feelings are not as intense as they may be with other people.

Even as adults, men and women still want to be taken care of, and many of us balk at the idea of committing ourselves to the often multiple grim realities of responsibility and adulthood. This inability to accept adult responsibility contributes to our romantic fantasies, in which we are completely and effortlessly cared for.

And that takes us back to our childhood.

Some of the most popular love songs could also be describing the mother/infant relationship, i.e., Leanne Rimes, "How Do I Live without You?" or Celine Dion's "I'm Everything I Am Because You Love Me." We're often pulled back to that blissful, chronic state of infantile helplessness. In other words, we hope when we marry, our childhood needs and wishes will be met.

These powerful fantasies and wishes underscore our deep yearning for an intimate connection to another person. This is ultimately who we want and hope we will end up with when we finally fall in love, choose our mate, and get married.

The characteristics of a person's attachments exist the day a person is born. In every romantic relationship our adult attachment style mimics the way a baby feels toward his or her mother, who is usually the main caregiver. Lovers can also see each other as a child that needs to be taken care of. From the crib to the tomb, this biological behavioral system governs our close relationships. And there is no adult relationship closer or that has more expectations placed on it than the marital relationship.

Freud viewed love from the perspective of the sexual drive and theorized that love and sexuality are rooted in infancy. A person's first love is his mother. The mother/first-love object provides the infant with not only food and nourishment, but also with a supply of sexual pleasure that he or she will later on seek from his or her adult lover. Freud looks at adult love and sexuality as an extension or rediscovery of motherly love.

According to researchers Arthur Aron and Elaine Aron, authors of *Love and the Expansion of Self: Understanding Attraction and Satisfaction,* love can be viewed as an expansion of the self. We are attached to others because they will help us be everything we can be, which, in addition to familiarity, is a major prediction of attraction. In the beginning of a relationship, similarity draws us to a person, helping us to feel familiar with and in sync with him or her.

Many people in the psychological community believe the unconscious mind plays the most significant role in who we fall in love with. Some profess that we fall in love because the unconscious mind believes it has found the partner who will finally make up for both the emotional and psychological damage we experienced in our youth, thus making us whole again. According to psychologist Dr. Harville Hendrix, from the moment we are born we are complicated and dependent beings who continue to have an ever-changing circuit of needs. Freud noted correctly that humans are "insatiable beings and no parent, no matter how devoted, is able to respond perfectly to all of these changing needs."

FAIRY TALES

Fairy tales and folklore also influence our ideas about love, marriage, and relationships. The attractiveness of many myths and legends comes from the basic human needs and experience they reflect.

One of the major themes in many legends is love and marriage. The most appealing characters are the heroes and heroines. The typical hero is the knight in shining armor while the leading female character tends to be the passive princess, waiting for that one special man to rescue her and carry her off into the sunset. What is of note is that most of these myths and legends are written by men. The knights, for instance, were often murderers and rapists. But these myths embody the male fantasy of what men want women to be and how men want to be viewed by women, as heroes who transform women and so become their saviors.

Almost every little girl wants to be a fairy-tale princess. My 2½-year-old daughter is going through this phase right now. On the most fundamental of levels these princess stories, such as Cinderella, are tales of transformation. Most of them are about turning one kind of girl into someone fantastically different, which is also a common thematic element in books, television, and film. Today there's a huge appetite for these kinds of stories among viewers of "reality" TV for example, *The Bachelor, The Bachelorette,* and *Extreme Makeover,* to name just a few.

The princess theme or syndrome is a story of social mobility, the idea that a women rises or climbs socially by virtue of the man she chooses to be attached to. It's not politically correct or progressive but nevertheless still holds credence today. There is still a princess attitude, if you will, among some girls and young women—that marrying well, especially financially well—will lead to the life of a princess.

The conflict is that the princess has a fundamentally passive role: She must wait to be chosen. In abusive relationships, it is often this very power imbalance that contributes to and in some cases exacerbates the violence and mistreatment in an intimate partnership. Sleeping Beauty is probably the most extreme story of the passive-role princess; she does absolutely nothing but sleep yet is transformed into a princess and lives happily ever after with her prince.

So what's the psychological appeal of such fairy tale romances? It doesn't matter what time period these stories are set in or what professional choices the hero or heroine makes. After the "Once upon a time . . ." opening, there later comes that much anticipated magical moment in any great fairy tale (just like in real-life romance): the perfect ending, when the couple walks into the sunset to finally . . . "Live happily ever after." The happily-ever-after is always there to look forward to. This firmly engrained idea can actually blind some people and help them stay in relationships that are potentially damaging, even lethal.

Fairy tales and romance are intimately linked and reflect both our deep wishes and deep fears. The fairy tale ends with the prince and the princess marrying and riding off into the sunset to start a new and amazing life together as husband and wife. Their life is full of promise, romance, and above all love. The problem is that no one tells us how it happens, why it succeeds, or if in fact it does. It alludes to this notion that true love is effortless and automatic if it is right and meant to be. Again, a major falsehood when it comes to real-life relationships.

Although few women expect to literally marry a royal prince, subconsciously they have assimilated these culturally essential messages. They transfer the fairy tale fantasies into real life and exalt acquiescence to male power, believing marriage to be not only an ideal state, but the ultimate domain toward which a woman should aspire. This idealization reflects a cultural attitude toward marriage and maternity as not only praiseworthy but predestined.

So fairy tales, aside from encouraging fantasies, also transmit romantic myths that encourage women to internalize ultraconservative aspirations which include what our real sexual functions should be within a male-influenced society. Interesting that this cultural fairy tale idea is closely linked with the evolutionary perspective of the primary function of marriage, which is to raise strong offspring so a man and woman can continue to spread their genes.

In Beauty and the Beast, the Beast's magical transformation into a devastatingly handsome prince makes it possible for Belle to have a love affair that is no longer grotesque. The story exemplifies the female hope that one can change a man's dark side with the right kind of love. Other characters, Cinderella and Sleeping Beauty, are rewarded for dreamily waiting for their prince and their patient servitude, while the Beast's transformation rewards Belle for accepting traditional female virtues.

Marriage serves as a bridge between these worlds of fantasy and reality. "Once upon a time" pulls us into a world of timeless fantasies and wish fulfillment with the wedding ceremony placing a person back into a more contemporary reality.

"Once upon a time" is then superimposed on the reality of marriage and becomes a major influence shaping a woman's experience and ideas on what her part of marriage should be. So again, even though women do not expect a fairy godmother to transform their rags into couture ball gowns, marriage is a state sought by many women. Women often expect or want marriage to provide them with happy domesticity, complete with a doting male to rescue them from the future dangers of life.

As illogical as these fantasies may be, in real life it is often true that romantic myth rather than actual experience influences women's expectations of men and marriage. If she cannot be a "real" princess, a woman can at least hope to become a sheltered wife, admired by a "prince of a man" who gives her children and maintains a happy home.

Even today many women still internalize romantic patterns and ideas that reference ancient tales. Although most women are aware that men are not princes and, in fact, some are unchangeable beasts, there still remains a deep-seated longing and female dream of the "perfect and fabulous man." Some believe as long as women buy into these romantic ideas they will be even more vulnerable to deceptions and disillusionments.

The dedicated romantic, or in extreme cases romantic obsessive, will reconstruct her reality into unsubstantiated, self-deluding fantasies by overlooking flaws and vehemently clinging to the more glorious aspect of matrimonial life. In the most severe cases, this rose-colored-glasses approach to a relationship can be devastating or even lethal for a woman (think Laci Peterson).

Everyone wants to have a love that is more powerful than anyone or anything in the world, and that is precisely what romance novels and soap operas deliver. An amazingly handsome, sexy, intelligent, and empathic man falls madly in love with a fiercely independent and beautiful young woman. They tease each other and flirt and eventually make mad, passionate love. The story concludes with a proposal or wedding, sometimes a baby, and they live happily ever after—the end.

The heroes in these romances are not ashamed of their desires, and their heroines are flattered by them. The relationship is held together by butterflies-in-your-stomach, breathless, passionate love. Women want all of this. They are drawn to these stories of seduction and passion. Soap operas and reality TV shows explore these themes of romance, and finding one's only true love appeals to audiences. These are modern examples of how we believe the right relationship can transform our lives, so they can resemble the lives in the fairy tale romances we so desperately admire.

SOUL MATE

According to the Zohar, a mystical commentary on the Torah, "forty days before conception a *bat kol* (heavenly voice) calls out that this one is destined to partner with that one." The noted Kabalist Isaac Luria further expands on this idea by stating that each of us is a part of different soul types and that certain soul types are more likely to connect than others.

The concept of the soul mate is another powerful idea that influences romance and who we want as a marital partner. Today, some believe in the esoteric notion that a soul mate is a person whom you have shared several lifetimes with through reincarnation. Others share the belief of the ancient Greek philosopher Plato, who opined that a soul mate is a person's "other half."

Today people all over the world embrace the idea that we are all searching for someone to complete us and make us whole, much like the hero played by Tom Cruise in the film *Jerry Maguire*. Lines such as "you complete me" and "you had me at hello" underscore the theme of finding the one and only perfect person designed especially for us, someone to share this journey of life with.

Most people think that a soul mate will accept and love every part of our personality, and that therefore life with a soul mate will be natural and effortless. I often hear disgruntled married patients in my office talk about how frustrated they are when a spouse does not know what they want and need, even if they have not shared or stated just what it is they need from that spouse.

The soul mate concept is a compelling one. Our soul mate is supposed to share our deepest thoughts and longings no matter what goes wrong around us. We are supposed to feel safe around this person who makes our life seem worth living. There is a divine grace surrounding the soul mate connection.

The dictionary defines soul mates as two persons compatible with each other in disposition, point of view, or sensitivity; between whom there is a deep affinity and temperamental harmony. Our perceptions of a soul mate and love relationships are largely based on movies, books, television, and fairy tales. Hollywood reinforces their notions of fate and soul mates, often examining the idea that people are effortlessly drawn together by destiny or fate, carrying over their love even after death.

Such notions of love and romance can be very misleading, because they present only part of the picture of what relationships are all about. To make the story more appealing, we see only the harmonious or marketable aspects of relationships with the underscoring theme that if we could just find our other half we could then reach true bliss and harmony.

According to psychologist Erich Fromm, "the desire for interpersonal fusion is the most powerful striving in man. It is the most fundamental passion. It is the force which keeps the human race together, the clan, the family, the society."

Why is this pull for a soul mate so powerful and universal? Well, logically, it stems from a place that we all have experienced, the womb. The intrauterine bonding occurrence is probably the most organic and influential experience we will ever have. Although it predates language and therefore can't necessarily be described in words, this experience is registered in each person's psyche.

A remarkable body of research suggests that the unborn child is aware, feeling and remembering what happens during those nine months which mold and shape its personality and ambition. Many believe that consciousness exists from the moment of conception—from the sixth month on, a fetus can hear, remember, and according to some even learn.

The womb is a child's very first experience of the world, and how he or she experiences it plays a major role in who this child will be both in character and temperament. While in utero everything the fetus needs is provided: food, oxygen, security, and safety. Nothing needs to be said or done; it's all automatic. When you think about it, this is the feeling state that finding a soul mate ideally should give us, a feeling of oneness and of automatically being taken care of.

As previously discussed, relationships, especially marital relationships, once were more for practical and economic reasons. Societal pressures dictated that couples, no matter what they were feeling, were supposed to stay together. This is certainly not the way things are today. People are following their hearts and their gut feelings when choosing the kind of partner and relationship they think is best for them. We expect a lot from marriage, and if a relationship is not meeting our needs, then a marriage is likely to end.

As a result of cultural brainwashing, we are programmed to believe that we need to find that one perfect person to meet all of our needs for the rest of our lives. This, of course, is impossible. But many of us still strive for it and believe we have failed if our expectations are not met. This distorted idealism and over-the-top expectation can set one up for major disappointment. For the fragile or disturbed mind, this disappointment can lead to violence and murder.

• • •

SPOUSAL violence has been well documented throughout history (think Henry VIII). Women were viewed as nothing more than property, the home was the man's castle, and women were to worship the man or face the consequences.

In past societies, getting rid of an inadequate wife was considered a legal right. Early Roman law allowed a man to beat, divorce, or murder his wife for the slightest offense, from dishonoring him to threatening his property rights. During the Middle Ages, when spousal violence was systemic, women who sought advice from their local priest were told only to be even more devoted and obedient to their husbands to win their approval, and hopefully lessen the abuse.

If the wife sought a divorce she could be beaten or killed, so she often had little choice but to grin and bear the abuse. However, in some instances, women fought back. For a woman the murder of a husband was, in some cases, a reflection of a societal need for an adequate divorce system, her unspoken defense: "Society gave me no other choice."

Today, there are plenty of choices for men and for women. Yet as you read through the ten motivations and triggers I found behind these murders, you will see that some people are unable to cope via modern-day resolutions, and in the end resort to handling their problems the old-fashioned way, through violence and murder.

2

The Betrayal/ Abandonment Killer

THE betrayal/abandonment murder is frequently referred to as a "crime of passion." These killers are not typical criminals. Instead they tend to be everyday people. The violent act in these instances is one of impulse where the killer doesn't weigh the consequences of his or her actions and is unaware of the impact of his or her actions due to the intensity of these emotions.

These crimes are not encouraged by monetary gain nor are they premeditated. When a murder of this kind is being committed, the ability to think clearly is momentarily suspended, and the id takes full rein over the human heart and mind. A combination of rage and primitive, deep-seated emotions replaces all judgment and restraint and gives way exclusively to unbridled release. Broken hearts, unbearable betrayal, and a deadly separation anxiety, all spurred by jealousy, are the emotional culprits for this type of murder. In fact, jealousy is one of the top three motives for nonaccidental homicides and also tends to be a primary motive for killing partners as well as romantic rivals. The triggers are learning about an affair or the end of a relationship.

Jealousy, and the feelings of betrayal and abandonment that follow, is often the dangerous counterpart of romantic love. Jealousy arises when an important relationship is threatened by a rival, whether real or imagined. It is a powerful emotion that has inspired many novels, drama, art, poetry, and operas. Some psychotherapists believe jealousy is more prominent in cultures that attach great social importance to marriage and approve of sexual gratification only within marriage. Jealousy is also found in cultures that place a high priority on personal property.

During the 1990s evolutionary psychologists applied Darwin's theory of human behavior to a novel theory that suggested that jealousy might have given us a fitness advantage in our ancestral environment.

Jealousy, like many emotions associated with mating, is different in men than in women. University of Texas professor of psychology Dr. David Buss, as well as several other researchers in his field, observed that a specific set of brain circuits influences our emotional reaction to danger and threats within the contexts of sexual relationships. According to these researchers, this process makes men more naturally inclined to be jealous over a mate's *sexual* infidelity while it makes women naturally inclined to be jealous over a mate's *emotional* infidelity. Some think that men assume that if a woman is having sex with a man it is because she is in love with him. Women tend to believe that men can have sex without being emotionally in love, so sexual infidelity does not necessarily mean that the man they care about is in love with his other partner. (Researchers have also pointed out that women and men who are struck by jealousy are often correct in believing that infidelity is taking place.)

The killers in this sort of crime, who are experiencing intense emotions, often view themselves as the doomed protagonists in a love tragedy gone terribly wrong where the saying *"If I can't have you, then nobody can"* is the theme song.

Such was the case of CLARA HARRIS, who wanted to "have it all" but instead gave it all up when, in July 2002, the married mother of two killed her husband David. Her weapon of choice was her Mercedes.

Clara had caught David, age forty-four, cheating with his assistant, and, following an ugly confrontation Clara repeatedly ran him over. The horrific act was caught on video and shocked a nation.

Up to that time theirs was, by most accounts, a perfect marriage. Both were dentists, having met in dental school in 1991. They married a year later, on Valentine's Day.

"I found the one God had reserved for me," Clara, age forty-four, once said.

They worked side by side, building a very successful practice in the suburbs of Houston, Texas, which allowed them to live in a palatial home in a gated community. They owned property in Colorado and vacationed often, usually to tropical locales. By 1998 they decided to start a family and Clara gave birth to twin sons. Life for David and Clara couldn't have been better. Or so everyone thought.

In reality, something was terribly wrong.

By 2002 David had taken a lover, Gail Bridges, a divorced mother of two and one of his dental assistants. The affair had continued for several months when David, confronted by Clara, finally admitted to his infidelity. He even described the affair to his wife in intimate detail.

Angry but resolute, Clara wanted to remain in the marriage and demanded that David end the affair. He said he would, but Clara didn't believe him and hired a private investigator, who tracked David and his lover to the luxurious Nassau Bay Hilton in the suburb of Clear Lake. It was the same hotel where the Harrises had married ten years earlier.

Tipped off by the private investigator, Clara arrived at the hotel with David's teenage daughter from his first marriage, Lindsay, age sixteen. They phoned upstairs to David, who came down minutes later. As he exited the elevator accompanied by Gail, they were surprised by Clara, who lunged at Gail, tearing at her shirt and screaming, "You bitch—he's my husband!"

Clara then turned to David and cried, "I hate you" before calling out into the lobby for everyone to hear that her husband was sleeping with another woman. Embarrassed and upset, David had heard enough. He took Gail's arm and headed for the front doors but was stopped by Clara and Lindsay. Enraged, David put his hand on Clara's forehead and pushed her down onto the floor, humiliating her. He then walked outside into the parking lot and escorted Gail to her car.

Clara quickly got back on her feet. Somewhat disoriented, she collected herself and was guided by hotel personnel to the parking lot and her Mercedes. She calmly got in the car, turned on the engine, and, as Lindsay slid into the passenger seat, pressed her foot on the gas, aiming the car for David, who was comforting Gail as they stood next to her Lincoln Navigator.

David didn't see Clara coming until the last moment. He pushed Gail inside her car as Clara plowed into him at forty miles per hour. He was catapulted twenty-five feet into the air and into an adjacent parking lot, where he lay motionless on the pavement, moaning from intense pain.

Clara, however, wasn't finished.

To the shock and horror of all watching, Clara sped her car over a concrete median into the adjacent parking lot, once again aiming directly for her husband. With Lindsay still in the passenger seat screaming for Clara to stop, she proceeded to run over

David again, and again, and again, circling the car over different parts of his body, crushing his legs, ribs, and head. The private investigator, sitting nearby in a parked car, captured the grisly event on tape. When Clara was finally finished she got out of her car and, in a final burst of anger, leaned over her husband's mangled, crushed body as he exhaled his last breath.

"See what you made me do!" Clara screamed.

It was the final act in a marriage Clara believed at the outset was the one she had wished for her entire life. Clara wanted the "perfect" husband, the "perfect" family, as well as the "perfect" successful career. For a while she fulfilled that dream, or so it seemed.

Clara was a former beauty queen, accomplished dentist, and mother of two who worked side by side with her adored husband. Their hard work resulted in luxuries reserved for only the lucky few. Unfortunately her life scenario culminated far from the picture-perfect storybook image she had worked so hard to create, and her dream crashed to a halt.

What would make such an intelligent and accomplished woman take such a fatal turn for the worse? What made Clara Harris do what most women would never do? After all, not many women who catch their husbands having affairs end up killing them. What was in Clara Harris's history that would transform her understandable jealousy into a murderous pathology?

CLARA Harris was born in Colombia. She lost her father at the young age of six and was raised by her struggling single mother. Life was difficult at best, but in adulthood, after attaining great success, Clara exclusively credited *her father* for her career as a dentist even though she had but a vague memory of him. The fact that she attributed her success to her father revealed that she had a deep longing for him as well as a deep longing to have an important male figure in her life. Not having a father left Clara prone to feeling abandoned, which ultimately made her vulnerable to committing murder under the right circumstances.

Without a male figure in her life she overly romanticized what it would be like to have one, and this engendered a narcissistic personality disorder that served as a defense against feeling worthless, abandoned, and unlovable. Clara's major childhood loss sparked a hyperactive sensitivity and persistent fear of losing men, especially the man she ultimately chose to make her own. This preoccupation manifested itself through extreme jealousy and would create what Harris feared most: losing the person she so loved and cherished.

Clara was a beauty queen, an achievement driven by her enormous need to be loved and valued. Winning a beauty pageant is the ultimate symbol of female success, one that signifies a woman's desirability to men. For Clara, this enabled her to hide her deep-rooted feelings of being an outsider, feelings developed over years of living without a father, a deprivation that produced an overwhelming attachment hunger for a romantic relationship. Attachment hunger is a normal need to attach or bond to another and originates from our unconscious desire to re-create the peaceful, euphoric, and omnipotent feelings we experienced as infants when we were totally dependent on our mothers. If this attachment hunger becomes overwhelming, a person can acquire the power to distort reality, which can lead to obsessive behavior in relationships, as opposed to a more normal desire for intimacy.

Clara's statement "I found the one that God had reserved for me" underscores her highly romanticized view of love. Clara believed that her husband would make all of her dreams for happiness finally come true, that David was her "one" true love and would finally make her feel fulfilled and complete. Juxtaposed against this ideal state was a deep-seated, psychological preoccupation with the childhood loss of a loved one. Clara's unconscious fear triggered the ill fate of her relationship with David, leaving her with only a shattered dream, which echoed the youthful loss of her father. Because of her overdependency, Clara's love for David was filled with profound insecurity and abnormal possessiveness. Abnormally jealous lovers tend to be:

- Always anxious when their partners are not present.
- Worry constantly about what their partners are doing if they're not in sight.
- Give their partners the third degree all the time.

This type of behavior by one partner can make the other partner feel smothered or even held hostage.

David and Clara were initially attracted to each other's similarities. Both were bright, ambitious dental students who seemed to have the same goals in life, but as with any intimate relationship, the fantasy of sameness gave way to reality. On an unconscious level Clara hoped "if you are identical to me, then you won't leave me." But the truth is that a partner simply cannot be one's identical mirror image. For a narcissistic personality who has a pathological fear of being abandoned, this reality would be too much of a disappointment to tolerate. Clara Harris viewed marriage as the ultimate source of redemption, as a means of healing all of her psychological and emotional wounds. Instead her marriage destroyed her, and her husband.

David Harris, after being caught by Clara at the hotel, was certainly not the most remorseful cheating husband in the world. He had the poor judgment to humiliate his wife further by push-

ing her to the floor and then walking his lover to her car, dismissing Clara's feelings of intense pain and agony. He no longer cared about her outrageous and dramatic outbursts.

For Clara, catching David with another woman was an emotional wound just too much to bear. Old feelings of being worthless and abandoned were awakened. The only response that made sense to her was to destroy the source of the pain. If Clara were better developed emotionally and had mastered the narcissistic stage of development, she would not have seen her husband as an extension of herself. Instead, David would have represented a separate and distinct person from whom she could separate. But when David left her and chose someone else, he confirmed her deepest fears, and once again, Clara felt worthless and unloved. Her response left her husband, the one that God reserved for her, dead.

During her trial in February 2003, Clara claimed she hit David with the car only once and that it had been an accident. The prosecution alleged that Clara had intentionally killed her cheating husband in a fit of jealousy and rage.

It's clear that Clara Harris did not really mean to kill her husband. She loved him more than life itself, and he knew that. Without David, life for Clara felt meaningless, empty, and perhaps most of all terribly lonely. She just wanted to stop the pain. The intensity of the sorrow he caused her was just too much to bear. He knew how vulnerable she was when it came to love, and he'd promised never to hurt her or to leave her. She believed him. How could he betray her this way? The rage and pain were so intense the only way to make them go away was to strike him down. He was strong. He would survive. He always did. She was the weak one. Because of her weakness, she could never kill him. The anger and anguish took over. All she could think about was eliminating the pain. Didn't David know that the pain was killing her?

Driving over his body gave Clara the illusion she could stop her husband from hurting and torturing her. She couldn't reconcile her murderous, rageful feelings with a man she still loved and didn't want to hurt. All she wanted was for things to be right, like they were in the beginning. And since she loved him, in her mind killing him was an accident, nothing more. There's no doubt David and Clara loved each other when they first met. But unknown to David, a fiery personality such as Clara's can be dangerous when the rose-colored glasses fade.

While Clara Harris acted swiftly upon learning of her husband's affair, BETTY BRODERICK let her emotions simmer over several years before her actions resulted in death.

The Broderick story is perhaps one of the most overpublicized and discussed cases of betrayal and abandonment. It's a story that follows the disintegration of a woman spurned and obsessed, and whose final act was one of murder.

Betty was a college student in New York when she met her future husband Dan, a premed student, at a Notre Dame football game. The pair dated for several years, became engaged and married in April 1969. Less than a year later Betty gave birth to the first of her four children, and the couple soon moved to Massachusetts, where Dan would attend Harvard, changing his career focus from medicine to law.

Betty helped support her husband during those early years, taking various jobs day and night to pay the rent and buy the food. In 1973 the young family moved to Los Angeles, and then soon after to San Diego, where Dan took a job as a junior partner with a local law firm. Overwhelmed by the crushing debt of her husband's student loans, Betty continued to work, teaching religious classes and earning her real estate license, her salary helping to keep the family solvent.

By 1979, following the birth of their fourth child Rhett, Dan had formed his own law firm and was quickly becoming one of the more successful attorneys in southern California. His success eventually led to a seven-figure salary, which allowed Betty to stay at home and fully devote herself to their children. Her hard work, devotion, and support of her husband, she believed, had finally paid off. But despite the appearance of an "idyllic" marriage, all was not well with the Brodericks. While Betty may have thought she and Dan were partners for life, Dan had other ideas. He often worked late into the evening, socializing with other attorneys at local pubs. His affinity for pubs resulted in one explosive confrontation with Betty while on a family vacation, when Dan spent more time in the local bar than with his family.

Dan was thought by many to be cold and distant, and as hard as she tried, Betty felt she could not please him. Friends could easily see changes in her demeanor at the end of the day when it came time for Dan to return home from work. Betty would transform from happy and easygoing to nervous, even afraid.

As Dan's law practice prospered, his marriage faltered. By 1983, and after fourteen years of marriage to Betty, Dan's attention was diverted toward another woman. Her name was Linda Kolkena, and Dan first spotted her at a party he attended with Betty. Linda was only twenty-one, but Dan was so smitten he soon hired her as his personal assistant. It wasn't long after they met that Betty began to suspect something was wrong. She'd catch her husband sneaking away to call Linda on the phone, and he'd even call her during family vacations. During one trip to England, Betty discovered that Dan had sent Linda flowers. While away with the children on a camping trip that summer,

Betty could not reach her husband on the phone. Upon her return Betty finally blurted her concerns about the pretty assistant, but Dan denied that anything illicit was going on, calling his wife paranoid and insecure.

After a surprise visit to her husband's office, Betty finally learned the truth. She arrived unannounced bearing gifts to celebrate his thirty-ninth birthday. But Dan was gone, and so was his assistant. They had left for lunch and never returned. Betty walked into Linda's office and saw a portrait of Dan there. Incensed, and believing that her husband was having an affair with his assistant, Betty drove home and pulled out all of Dan's expensive, tailor-made suits. She threw them into a pile in the backyard, poured gasoline on them, and set the clothing afire. When Dan returned home Betty confronted him about his assistant, but Dan again denied he was having an affair. It wasn't long after that confrontation that Dan finally admitted the truth, that indeed he was involved with his assistant and he wanted a separation from Betty.

OVER the next several years the Betty Broderick story was one of rejection, violence, verbal abuse, and finally murder. Feeling scorned and unable to accept the loss of her husband and a life she loved and felt she deserved, Betty became more and more erratic. And given Dan's stature within the legal community and knowledge of the court system, he saw to it that Betty was thwarted at every turn, which added to Betty's anger and resolve, and to her increasingly bizarre and dangerous behavior.

After announcing his intention to seek a divorce, Dan moved the family into a spacious rented home, claiming repairs were needed at their own home. But when the repairs were completed Dan returned there, alone. Enraged, Betty would visit and vandalize the home. On one occasion she took a chocolate cream pie, which had been baked by Linda as a gift for Dan, and smeared it across Dan's suits and the very bed she'd once shared with him. On another occasion she threw a wine bottle through a window.

Dan obtained a restraining order against Betty, which infuriated her even more, especially since the separation wasn't anything she wanted. She certainly didn't want a divorce and told friends that her difficulties were all caused by her husband. He was the one manipulating their break-up and who had cast her into a rental home and who made *her* appear to be the bad guy while he appeared to be the victim. Her psyche degenerating, Betty struck again during the Christmas season of 1985. With Dan and Linda's relationship already publicly acknowledged, the couple took Dan's children away for a holiday vacation. Betty, alone, once again broke into her former home and destroyed holiday gifts left under the tree. Even after moving into a new home, Dan could not rid himself of Betty, who drove her van through Dan's front door. Betty was taken to a mental hospital and sedated. She was released after three days.

For the next three years, despite numerous restraining orders, Betty continued to harass her estranged husband and his girlfriend, often leaving dozens of profanity-laced messages on his home answering machine. And with each message Dan would withdraw alimony money for every obscene word heard on the tape. He also began to deduct higher amounts, as much as $1,000, for other misbehavior, such as taking the children without advance warning. Even the children, who Betty said she loved more than anything else in the world, became pawns in her continuing battle with her husband.

Betty's anger had boiled over into obsession and torment by January 1989. Their divorce now final, she was completely crushed by the courts, which awarded custody of the children to

Dan and left Betty with only $30,000 in cash. The final blow came three months later, when Dan announced his engagement to Linda.

On November 5, 1989, Betty Broderick awoke before dawn and drove to Dan's home. She used a key she secretly took from her daughter to let herself inside. She walked upstairs, a .38 caliber revolver in hand, and into Dan's bedroom, where he and Linda were sleeping.

Betty fired, killing them both.

Her first trial ended in a hung jury. Her second trial, in October 1991, saw Betty convicted on two counts of second-degree murder. She was sentenced to thirty-two years to life and is eligible for parole in 2011.

FOR Betty Broderick, it was life imitating art as she appeared to take her fatal marital cues from the movie *Fatal Attraction.* In this movie a married man, played by Michael Douglas, engages in a brief but exciting sexual fling with a colleague, played by Glenn Close. Although the Douglas character initially finds the relationship erotic and exhilarating, he quickly decides to break it off so he won't ruin his marriage. But his lover refuses to accept this rejection and instead begins relentlessly stalking him, believing she can still win back his love and rejuvenate their "special" relationship. It finally escalates to the point where one evening she breaks into her former lover's house, holding a large kitchen knife.

Instead of being the obsessed lover, Betty Broderick was the obsessed estranged wife who could not let her husband or her marriage go.

As noted earlier, statistically speaking, women kill at far lower rates than men. But when they do kill it is often due to jealousy and abandonment and the feelings of betrayal caused by rejection. Clara Harris and Betty Broderick are definitely not the first women to be accused of murdering their spouses in a jealous rage.

Betty was a traditional woman of her time who believed in the all-encompassing romantic fantasy, the one where you meet and marry your true love and then live happily ever after, eventually walking into the sunset together. Betty idealized marriage and what it could do for her as a person. Her only goal in life was to become a beloved wife and mother. Unfortunately she married a man who did not share her sentiment or dream, at least not with her.

At the beginning of her marriage she was very much on her way to making her dreams come true, serving as the ideal wife for a fiercely ambitious husband by placing his professional aspirations first, something that many women of her generation did, willingly or not. They supported their husbands' rise to success, believing one day they would gloriously share in that success. And as long as Betty worked hard alongside her husband and supported his dreams, she could feel safely connected to him. After all, how could Dan leave such a valuable life partner? But like many young romances, the happy ending she had scripted in her mind was not meant to play out in real life the way she wanted it to.

While Betty believed she had found a charming, handsome, and intelligent man in Dan Broderick, he had some narcissistic qualities. People like Dan tend to have a grandiose sense of themselves. They want to be recognized as special, important, and unique. Their preoccupation with unlimited success often helps them to achieve that success. After all, it's what they already believe to be true about themselves.

Narcissistic people often need excessive praise and admiration and they often find it in socially charming ways. Narcissism and infidelity are often linked. People who marry people with narcissistic tendencies can be in for a rough road with lots of suffering. Such spouses tend to be self-absorbed with an amazing sense of entitlement exacerbated by a lack of empathy for the emotional harm they cause others. Betty Broderick was certainly unprepared for the dark side of a failed relationship with a narcissist. And that failure appeared to strike at the very core of her being.

Betty described her husband as intermittently abusive, but as long as she was able to be the kind of wife who could help him get to where he wanted to go, she was able to stick around. But as soon as she didn't meet his needs or was not a reflection of who he wanted to be, she was dismissed and left. By her account, he did very little to consider her feelings or experiences during their marriage, but as long as Dan was providing her with what appeared to be family stability and a successful life, Betty could accept his behavior as part of the package of marrying an extremely successful man.

She also felt that as long as she was doing so much for their family and his career, she would be indispensable to her husband. Dan Broderick's name-brand suits, late nights out with the guys, plus the financial burdens he placed on his wife were all okay in his mind as long as he was benefiting and supported in living the life he felt destined for.

Contrary to comments Betty once made on *Oprah* in 1992, there doesn't seem to be evidence of physical abuse, though she does appear to have been emotionally neglected. The marriage was not about her needs, unless her needs happened to be met while his were being considered and pursued. Although Betty didn't know it, she could have a place in Dan's life only as long as she helped him get where he wanted to go. That's probably why he agreed to marry her in the first place. On some level he sensed he could do what he wanted and she would be okay with that while providing him with a big family, another sign of his success.

What Dan was not prepared for was a woman who may

have appeared whole on the outside, but emotionally was more like a half a person. Without Dan in her life, Betty could not exist, feel lovable or even effectively okay in the world.

When we think about unrequited love, we don't tend to think of it within the context of a marital union. Once someone marries, we assume that there is some degree of reciprocity in the relationship. After Dan Broderick committed the ultimate betrayal and traded in his older wife for a new and improved model, a.k.a. the trophy wife, Betty turned into a stalker. A stalker is someone who continues a relationship when the other person is not at all interested in it. The pursuer often presses his or her need for more connection and intimacy while the object of the pursuit wants and desires more freedom and autonomy. The person engaged in this type of stalking behavior is often fixated, persistent as well as morbidly preoccupied. There is an obsessional nature to their behavior. When women stalk, they tend to do so in an attempt to achieve intimacy. Betty Broderick became an obsessional estranged lover, which makes up the largest category of pursuers/stalkers.

This category tends to consist of people who just cannot let go of the romantic relationship. Their entire sense of self-worth is caught up in the need for the other's love. Any evidence to the contrary is seen as an inconvenience to overcome. Through merging with the other person they view themselves as having a higher status in life, that is, "If somebody loves me, then I'm not so bad." The stalker's theme lyric could be "You're no one 'till someone loves you!" The most common motivator for the pursuit is a strong desire for reconciliation. When attempts to reconnect with a former lover become obsessive, the pursuer is usually labeled as love addicted.

While erotomaniacs (erotically obsessed people) are said to be more psychotic, believing they have a connection to the person that they are stalking when in reality they don't, estranged lovers are thought to be more psychopathic or personality disordered.

Betty's condition best fits into the diagnostic category of borderline personality disorder. According to the National Institute of Mental Health, this is a "serious mental illness characterized by pervasive instability in moods, interpersonal relationships, self-image and behavior. This instability often disrupts work and family life."

This diagnosis tends to affect 2–3 percent of the general population and is three times more likely to be found in women than in men. People with this diagnosis tend to become seriously self-destructive and ill in reaction to fears of abandonment. When frustrated they show rage and can become extremely devaluing. People diagnosed with this disorder tend to come from dysfunctional families, with erratic and often depressed mothers and fathers who are absent and/or have major character problems.

It's clear that on some level Dan sensed Betty's disturbance. It's also clear that at one point Betty fueled Dan's dependency needs, but later he felt smothered by her and overwhelmed by the feeling that something was lacking. Their breakup was actually years in the making, with Dan justifying, in his mind, reasons for staying with Betty: It would kill her if he left; It's not really that bad; It's going to change; It'll get better; fear of the unknown; even a precognition of how off balance she was. But once Dan met someone else who gave him the feelings he wanted to have and longed for, it became impossible for him to stay married to Betty.

The termination of this and most other relationships produces an overload of emotional stress which is often accompanied by a multitude of powerful feelings such as diminished self-esteem and self-worth, humiliation, depression, anger, and hurt. After repeated rejection and a fear that the former love relationship cannot be restored, the ditched lover seeks retribution and then may threaten to harm the former partner.

Of all of the types of stalkers/pursuers, the obsessed estranged lover, for the most part, is the most dangerous, often displaying a propensity for violence. These kinds of personalities, much like Betty Broderick, experience a sense of fusion with their lover along with a sense of urgency. They are overwhelmingly anxious about reciprocity. They tend to idealize their lover and feel insecure outside of the relationship. They experience extremes of happiness and sadness and often have impaired reality testing in the relationship. In a way, they are relationally incompetent. Their behavior is a maladaptive response to loneliness, social isolation, and social incompetence.

What makes them different from other people is their level of aggression and pathological narcissism. The chronic rejection challenges their idea about themselves that they are special, admired, superior, and in some way destined to be with the object of their pursuit. Betty Broderick's identity and self-esteem were dependent on her husband being married to her, and on her being a mother and being the wife of a prominent, successful, and desirable man. As long as Betty was married to Dan, she could dismiss her feelings of inferiority and lack of feeling like a whole person.

Feelings of grandiosity and pride trigger feelings of humiliation and shame that are defended against with rage, and the rage helps to stop the intolerable feelings of hurt. The intense anger is an attempt to fend off feelings of sadness because of the obsessive lover/stalker's inability to fend off feelings of loss and grief. Despite the various psychological deficits found in these people, they are often very motivated in their pursuit. These obsessed stalkers tend to be more educated and intelligent than comparison groups of stalkers. They also tend to be very manipulative and resourceful. Sometimes love-obsessed stalkers want to inflict terror and revenge, but most of the time they are unaware of the distress they are causing to the victims of their pursuit.

Betty Broderick didn't believe that she was having any impact on her former spouse at all, which is why she escalated the intensity of her actions. In her mind, Dan was going to listen to her, no matter what.

Pursuers such as Betty tend to be very egocentric, and more absorbed in their own thoughts and feelings than in the feelings of the one from whom they are seeking attention. They also tend to rationalize their behavior. Betty no doubt told herself that if Dan had not abandoned her, then she would not have had to try to reason with him in this unconventional and inconvenient way. If he would only admit how important she was to him and how important their love was, she would stop her behavior.

Dan could not and would not give his wife that validation, and as a result he paid with his life. According to an interview I had with Dr. Miriam Ehrenberg, adjunct professor of psychology at John Jay College of Criminal Justice, it is a huge narcissistic injury when a woman provides services for a man and invests herself in her husband's success but then is dismissed and unrecognized for what she did and how her support contributed to her husband's success. When such a woman is rejected, it leads to a feeling of being undervalued, used, and/or in some cases even imprisoned. It's a stark denial and a cold dismissal of what the woman has offered to the marital relationship.

Ehrenberg added that when husbands offer wives a materialistic accoutrement, at least that is something they can point to and say, "Look what I gave you, a mink coat, a diamond ring," and so on. It is this imbalance of power, Ehrenberg believes, that in some cases makes certain couples vulnerable to spousal homicide. The result is that the stalker's actions (at least in her own mind) can often be justified in the name of love. She feels that her honorable intentions justify her extreme actions. Such stalkers are also guided by a cultural script that promotes the idea that persistence encourages romantic success.

Love is believed to be one of the most important and exciting experiences a person can have in life. On the other hand, to be rejected by someone after you let him know over and over again who you are and how much you love him is particularly devastating to a person's self-esteem. It's as if the rejecter is saying, "Now that I really know you, I'm no longer interested in you."

Sometimes rejecters feel guilty for their lack of desire and inability to return the other person's loving feelings and affections. Unrequited love leads to a feeling of low self-esteem, and the need to protect one's self-esteem is basic and powerful. The rejected can feel inferior, unattractive, and unlovable. The later in the relationship the rejection comes, the more intense and powerful the humiliating message is. For Betty, this message was "You're old and not deserving of someone as attractive, wealthy, and successful as I am. You were fine on the way up, but now I can do better, so I will."

This is a particularly harsh message in a society that does not seem to value women as they age. Older women commonly fear being replaced by a younger model, a model perhaps capable of bearing children. Older, successful men may want to advertise their success by acquiring a young and glamorous wife. It's a signal that they have arrived and are doing well in the world.

Once Dan Broderick chose another woman to love, there was nothing else he could do for Betty other than die. Betty Broderick was going to make her husband keep at least one promise he made to her, a promise he made long ago when they stood before God. That was the promise of "till death do us part."

Betty loved him to death. He was hers whether he knew it or not. If he could not keep his promise in life she would have to help him keep it in death. Apparently the only way to make him keep his promise to be loyal to her was to kill him. Only then could she agree to move on. But even so, she was totally unprepared to live life without her husband.

With nothing to do now but think about her actions, I do think that Betty may well be far more intact and happier now, knowing that Dan is out of her life. Gone are her feelings of rejection. If she couldn't have a positive relationship with her husband, she needed to have a negative relationship with him.

On a final note, it's also interesting that Betty killed both Dan and Linda in their bedroom. In the unconscious the bedroom symbolizes sex and sexuality; in their case being in the bedroom could have led to Dan and Linda having children together, which would serve to devalue the one thing Betty felt she did so well, giving Dan beautiful children.

Dan's murder was a crime of passion, motivated by feelings of abandonment and betrayal. Betty couldn't believe, after all these years, that Dan wouldn't come home. Betty's version of reality was more powerful than the real reality. Dan was hers, only nobody but Betty seemed to know it. Now he would be linked with her forever.

3
The Control Killer

CONTROL killers are men and women who micromanage and monitor every action of their spouse or significant other, demanding to know the other's whereabouts at all times, who he or she talks to, socializes with, even what the other is wearing. They adopt this pattern of behavior because *they* feel so out of control. Sometimes the final act in such relationships is one of violence.

The victims of this type of homicide are married to or involved with long-term abusers, often male, and suffer severe and frequent abuse before they become victims of the ultimate abuse, murder. Many of these victims were often isolated and imprisoned in their own homes, psychologically abused, and made to feel worthless and unlovable, brainwashed to believe that she was to blame for her own victimization. That same victim, in part due to denial, believes at first that she can fix the unhealthy relationship. But that is not the case, as the abusive partner ultimately turned murderer projects feelings of self-hate and worthlessness onto his partner. And as long as the abuser maintains his violent status it is assured that he will never become the abused or victimized one. By maintaining the belief that his partner is damaged, he doesn't have to face up to his own personal feelings of failure or inadequacy.

These controlling behaviors are a defense against feeling vulnerable and out of control, which is the opposite of what they pretend to be. It's a very "all or nothing" or "black or white" type of thinking *("If you're worthless, then I'm not")*. The abuse escalates to murder when the abuser is reminded of his "worthlessness" and becomes pathologically or even delusionally jealous about his partner leaving for another lover or having an affair with someone else.

When the abused spouse finally decides to leave the relationship, the abandonment is the ultimate confrontation and reminder that the abuser is not in control of his life at all and he takes back his control by making himself right: *"You will never leave me!"*

SUCH was the case of DAVID BRAME of Tacoma, Washington.

David was Tacoma's chief of police while his wife Crystal was a stay-at-home mom, caring for the couple's two young children, Haley, eight, and David Jr., five, and supporting her busy, important husband.

David, forty-four, was a role model for the entire city. The son of a police officer, David rose through the ranks, from patrolman to sergeant to his appointment as the city's top cop. When he became chief of police in 2002, Crystal proudly stood by his side.

Despite the public perception of their marital bliss, all was not well with the Brames.

A year after David's promotion, Crystal filed for divorce, claiming her husband of eleven years was an obsessive, controlling presence in her life. Included among Crystal's allegations were that David refused to let her use their credit cards without permission; that he continually checked the car odometer, even after her trips to the grocery store; and that he had threatened her life. Crystal also alleged that her husband had a "ferocious temper," was emotionally unstable, and that on four occasions in 2002 he had tried to choke her, only to send her flowers afterward with a "heartfelt" apology. Crystal also claimed that David brandished his gun at her, a reminder that he was in control, and that he demanded changes in their sex life, particularly that he wanted to engage other partners in threesomes.

David responded with his own petition, alleging that Crystal scratched and bruised him during several fights in the mid-1990s.

Crystal's allegations, especially the troubling charges of domestic violence, were published in a local paper. Publicly humiliated, David was pressured by the local media and various city officials to resign. For David, giving up his badge and gun was tantamount to giving up one of his limbs, or worse, his life.

On April 26, 2003, two cars converged in a parking lot in Gig Harbor, an upscale suburban community. In one car was Crystal, in the other was David, who was accompanied by the couple's two children. Just minutes earlier Crystal was driving through town talking to her mother on her cell phone when she spotted David, who was driving with the children in his red Toyota. Crystal followed David into a parking lot. After spotting his wife, David left the children in his car, telling them he wanted to talk to their mother. Witnesses heard loud arguing followed by two gunshots. Crystal fell to the pavement, seriously wounded. David was slumped in the car. He had turned the gun on himself and was barely breathing. David died two hours later from the single shot to his head while Crystal hung on another week before succumbing to her head wound.

The murder/suicide shocked the city, and the nation: a police chief, in the prime of his career, committing an unspeakable crime. But as the months went by, more details emerged about the Brames' troubled marriage, David's violent history, and of disturbing signs David displayed which had been ignored.

David Brame was born and raised in Tacoma. He was athletic, playing baseball and basketball at Lincoln High School, where he was a member of the school's 1975 championship basketball team.

He graduated from college in 1980 with a degree in public administration and applied for a job with the Tacoma police department, which was to be expected since his father, older brother, and a cousin were all cops. But during the application process David failed one psychological test and marginally passed another. One psychologist described David as "defensive" and "deceptive." Another called David "somewhat apathetic, depressed, and emotionally over-controlled with self doubts." Despite their concerns, David was hired and joined the police department. During his career David was well liked, and his superiors commended him for his apparent good judgment and ability to deal with diverse community issues. He also began to accumulate commendations for street arrests. To those who knew him, he was, in the words of one friend, "a class act."

But below the public persona lurked a decidedly darker and troubled man. Unknown to but a few members of the department, David was accused of raping a woman in 1988. She was a juvenile counselor who worked with David and they had agreed to go out on a date. Following a quiet dinner at a local restaurant they returned to his home where, alleged the woman, David attacked her as they were sitting on a sofa. The woman claimed that David ignored her pleas to stop and then carried her to the bedroom where he threw her down, pulled her hair, and lifted her head so she could see his gun on a night table. After he raped her, David began to cry and apologized.

The woman later confided the rape to another police officer who scheduled a meeting between the woman and David. At the meeting David admitted to the rape and again apologized, saying he had begun counseling. The officer, a friend of David's, reported the rape to internal affairs, which began an investigation. But David denied the rape to police officials and was eventually cleared. Three years later, he met and married Crystal Judson.

A pretty brunette barely five feet tall, Crystal had graduated with honors from high school and had attended the University of Washington, majoring in criminal justice. She was twenty-three, nine years younger than David, when they married. It wasn't long before Crystal began to withdraw from her friends and family, becoming more sullen and introverted. And soon after she gave birth to her two children local shopkeepers would see Crystal scrounge for change when making purchases. She loved to shop, but she could not use the couple's credit cards without David's permission and she had to get David's approval before actually buying a coveted item, even a Christmas tree.

After eleven years of marriage, Crystal confided to close friends and her parents about David's abusive behavior. She had gained weight after giving birth to their children and he criticized her appearance. He'd also belittle her for not holding a job and always reminded her that he was the breadwinner. Worse still, David would control her every movement, marking every second of her day, demanding to know her whereabouts at all times. He also maintained fear and apprehension through daily physical and verbal abuse, often threatening to snap her neck.

For Crystal, the final straw was when David sought

changes in their sexual activity, nudging his wife to participate in diversions such as threesomes and foursomes.

Crystal finally summoned the courage to leave her husband, and in February 2003, without warning, Crystal and the children left the house and moved into her parents' home in a gated community in Gig Harbor. Over the next two months she began to make subtle changes in her life. She lost weight, and her friends and family saw a noticeable, and positive, difference in her personality.

In public David remained stoic. He sought professional counseling to handle the stress of his pending divorce, even attending an FBI seminar on emotional survival training for police officers. But privately he was falling apart, turning his rising anger toward his estranged wife, intimidating her family, and again threatening her life. Crystal's parents were so concerned about David's mental health that they insisted on being present whenever he picked up or dropped off the children before or after his weekend visitation.

The day before the murder/suicide David returned from a training conference in Las Vegas and picked up the children. The next morning he took the children first to karate class and then shopping while Crystal drove to Tacoma to attend a class on "What Children of Divorce Really Need." When she returned to Gig Harbor that afternoon, she spotted David's car and followed him into the parking lot. David told the children to wait in his car, walked over to Crystal's car, and sat in the driver's seat, which had been vacated by Crystal, who stood outside the car, scared and distant. At that moment David knew it was over, that she had made her decision, and there was nothing he could do about it. His anger, which had vacillated over the past few months between simmering and boiling, rose to the surface. Combined with the embarrassing disclosures in the newspaper, David was lost. There was only one way for him to retake control. Words were exchanged, then shouts from Crystal of "Oh, no, don't!"

The news was shocking, with Tacoma mayor Bill Baarsma telling a local television station he knew David as a "proud and loving father."

"They were a beautiful couple," said Baarsma.

AS in many marriages that turn out to be violent and controlling, Crystal and David seemed to be ideal partners at first. David was ambitious, but there was a sinister/dark side to this seemingly charming and engaging man.

Crystal was remembered fondly as being sweet and the type of person who worked hard to please people. Her friends remember her as a physically strong and self-confident woman, which is one of the reasons this tragedy was particularly devastating for the people who knew her well. Crystal was the last person anyone would have thought likely to shrink away and blend into oblivion. But like so many women who find themselves in abusive relationships, that is exactly what she did.

It's hard to identify abusive and controlling men, especially during the early part of a relationship and especially for a young, naïve, and hopeful twenty-three-year-old girl. Such men are frequently very seductive and sweep women off their feet with romantic sentiments, inducing an alluring and almost addictive sense of specialness in the person they are trying to win over. This euphoria at the beginning is the feeling everyone hopes for when they are dating someone they find interesting. At first, it appears that the object of affection has everything desired in a lover. Who wouldn't want to dive headfirst into a relationship that makes you feel sexually attractive and places you high on that proverbial pedestal? The problem is, as with most things in life, if something appears to be too good to be true, it usually is.

Controlling and abusive men often idealize their partner out of their own desperate need to be attached to someone who can heal them and make them feel better. They want and need their new mate to experience them as the best and most wonderful in every single way, the best lover, the best person, as well as a constant source of interest and fascination.

Of course people are fallible and flawed, so this "perfect" honeymoon period can last for only so long. Sooner or later, the idealized lover will fall from grace, only to disappoint the controlling partner and "prevent" his true needs from being met.

Control killers come from two main groups of spousal abusers: the common couple violence abuser and the patriarchal terrorism abuser. The common couple violence abuser is an occasional and unpredictable abuser who has volatile responses to the pressures of everyday life. His violence is motivated by a need to control a specific circumstance, as opposed to the violence of the patriarchal terrorism type, who wants to control the woman and the relationship by any means necessary. Men in this latter group tend to commit acts of abuse characterized by a strong need to be completely in charge of the relationship and to control the woman. The violence in these relationships is male to female and, as the relationship continues, the violence becomes more frequent and severe. Such males are determined to maintain their control by any means necessary, including physical violence and psychological abuse, the latter comprising sexual, emotional, and verbal abuse, as well as social and economic isolation.

Such men appear to have a problem with women achieving power, and their violent behavior is a result of the male entitlement and dominance represented in our society. These types of batterers and abusers are limited in their ability to feel attachment and empathy and have the most rigid and conservative attitudes about women. David fit this typology of patriarchal terrorism perfectly, especially since he exhibited problems with women way before he ever met and married Crystal.

Take, for example, the former coworker he was accused of raping. No amount of her begging and pleading with him would change his obsessional need to rape her. Although he told everyone he was getting counseling, the therapy obviously wasn't enough to help him with his destructive and self-destructive mode of operating. Men who rape women often do it to show their strength, masculinity, and virulence. This power motive often involves the perception that women are property and specifically the property of men, and the act of rape establishes that power.

David tried to establish control in a multitude of ways with Crystal. He emotionally abused her by calling her fat and telling her no man would ever want to be with her. He financially abused her by forcing her to account for every dime spent, and his constant checking up on her made it difficult for her to be with friends or family. She was, in effect, socially isolated. And toward the end of their relationship, he sought to engage in threesomes and foursomes, something he knew Crystal, a conservative mother of two, had no interest in pursuing.

Eventually Crystal could no longer justify the abuse, and the days of making excuses for David were over. She had a right to a nice life and she was going to try to make that happen. She missed having friends and feeling good about herself. But she was also aware that she was in danger. She knew it was not beyond David to want to harm her for leaving him. He pretty much told her as much. But his threats to kill her were not going to stop her this time.

According to evolutionary psychologists Margo Wilson and Martin Daly, violence against a female partner is often intended to prevent the partner from pursuing other romantic relationships. Men are often motivated to kill a spouse out of jealousy, especially if they are estranged and the commitment to the relationship is seen as tenuous or challenged.

Estranged male perpetrators are also more likely than estranged female partners to seek out, track down, and kill an ex-partner for leaving them. Unfortunately that was the case for David and Crystal. She left an abusive marriage and before long started to feel great about herself. But her burgeoning joy was short lived, as was the life of her estranged spouse, who turned the gun on himself.

Homicide is the only crime that regularly results in the criminal taking his or her own life following the act. Although people tend to view homicide and suicide as opposite ends of the spectrum, it is possible for someone to feel homicidal and suicidal at the same time. Such people are typically involved in a chaotic, frustrated, long-term intimate relationship and such relationships often vacillate between extreme feelings of anger and love. There can also be this idea that one person has been sexually unfaithful. The triggering event is often the separation from the spouse or love object. This separation can produce intense and severe depression, which increases the suicide risk factor. The murder/suicide is a consequence of a sense of unbearable powerlessness, a feeling a controlling spouse is trying all along to avoid having. The murderous act is viewed with guilt and shame after the perpetrator realizes the crime that he has committed. This then intensifies his suicidal impulse.

Others argue that the perpetrators of the murder/suicide are trapped in a vicious cycle of frustration-nurturance-frustration. So when the source of the frustration is killed, in this case Crystal, so is the source of nurturance. When the nurturance is lost the homicidal frustration increases, and then turns against the self in the form of suicide, as it did in David's case. We know that murder/suicides are not monolithic acts. These acts have many different dimensions. Sometimes murder/suicide is an outgrowth of guilt. In other cases, according to Wilson and Daly, it happens because the female becomes so much a possession or piece of property that she also needs to be taken along on the journey of death. In other cases murder/suicide may preserve the fantasy that the two lovers will remain together forever.

What is particularly interesting, statistically, is that, unlike men, women rarely kill themselves after killing their partner. When women kill, it's often to get away from their partner, to escape, not to take him along into eternity. Men are also prone to be more dependent on women for their sense of self and emotional connection since they often have difficulty developing intimate connections with friends and family, something most women develop early in life. Unlike women, men connect on a more practical/superficial level and rely on the women in their lives to provide emotional and social stability.

And finally, these homicides highlight the point that just because the relationship is over, it does not mean that the control or violence is over.

While most such acts are cold and calculated, I do not think this was so in David Brame's case. His act seemed to be carried out with about as much thought as a road rage incident. But David was unprepared for what it would feel like to see his wife and not have control of her and her choices. David was unable to tolerate his losses. He had to once and for all show Crystal who was the boss, even if it meant cutting off his own nose to spite his face. It had to be done; there was no other choice, at least for him, not at that moment.

ROBERT BIERENBAUM also felt there was no other choice.

On Sunday, July 7, 1985, his wife Gail, twenty-nine, disappeared without a trace following an argument in their New York apartment. The couple had been married for four years and, despite outward appearances, theirs was a marriage deeply fractured and marked by infidelity and abuse.

When they met in 1979, Gail was a college dropout who suffered from depression, liked to drink, and was dependent on drugs, particularly Quaaludes. She was one of three children who grew up in a pretty typical middle-class Long Island Jewish family. Although bright, she had little interest in school. Unlike her sister, Alyane, who was studious, reserved, and studying to be a lawyer, Gail was drifting through life without any clear goals or direction. She liked late-night parties, the wild-musician-type bad boys, and the drinking and drugging that often goes with the partying lifestyle. Gail was beautiful, sexy, and gregarious, but her outward beauty could not mask her depression and drug dependency.

She was living in an apartment with a male friend when she met Robert Bierenbaum. He was a budding doctor who piloted small planes in his spare time, spoke five languages, was a gourmet chef, and came from a well-to-do family from New Jersey. Robert was also a perfectionist, a young man who insisted on doing things his way.

Being that Gail was a twenty-three-year-old with low self-esteem, suicidal tendencies, and no direction in life, Robert seemed a perfect catch. Gail's family eagerly approved, hoping the union would set her on a straight and narrow path to success and happiness. Gail initially claimed she was smitten with Robert, who romanced her with night flights over the Manhattan skyline. But in reality the marriage didn't make much sense for Gail. She wasn't in love with Robert and worse, she didn't even find him attractive. Still, despite her reservations he was, after all, a doctor.

So they became a couple. At Robert's insistence Gail quit her job and moved into his apartment. But it wasn't long after they began cohabiting that troubling signs surfaced. Gail told her friends and family that Robert needed to be in control of every aspect of her life, from her weight to her hair. He also had a vicious temper and was irrational at times, leading to loud arguments, often over nothing of great consequence.

On one occasion, Gail claimed Robert attacked her after he unexpectedly returned home and caught her smoking a cigarette in their apartment. On another occasion Gail claimed he tried to drown her cat in the bathtub in a fit of jealousy. Both incidents were reported to police.

Dependent on her husband, Gail finished college, earning her B.A. and deciding to study for a Ph.D. in clinical psychology. Her graduation coincided with yet another violent turn of events as the couple drifted even further apart, with Gail seeking out and participating in numerous extramarital affairs. In 1983, just two years into their marriage, the physical abuse and constant verbal threats of violence escalated to the point where Robert sought psychiatric help, hoping to erase, or at least come to grips with, his demons. During his sessions, which would later be revealed, Robert admitted to having violent thoughts and tendencies toward his wife.

Concerned that the threats were serious, one of the doctors (with Robert's permission) exercised his Tarasoff duty, meaning that he warned Gail that she could be in serious danger. In his letter, the psychiatrist cited Robert's "characterological abnormalities." For her part, Gail briefly moved out of their apartment, but refused to sign the letter. Instead she returned to Robert and remained in the marriage as her husband was on his way to becoming a top-flight Manhattan surgeon.

But as soon as she returned the domestic violence resumed, and Gail's family pleaded with her to leave Robert. A month before she disappeared, Gail confronted her husband, demanding a divorce and threatening as leverage to publicize the letter from the psychiatrist warning that she was in danger. The letter, she said, would expose him as being psychotic, which would ruin his career.

The day she disappeared, neighbors heard them arguing yet again, with Gail confessing to her extramarital affairs and demanding a divorce. The following day Robert made several calls to Gail's friends and family, asking if they knew where she was. They all feared the worst.

The police were called and Robert told them that he and his wife had argued and she left the apartment. He then attended a nephew's birthday party in New Jersey, visited with a friend, and returned home later that night. But Robert left out one bit of crucial information, failing to tell investigators that he had rented an airplane from a New Jersey airport and he flew, alone, for two hours over the Atlantic Ocean.

Gail never returned home, and police classified her disappearance as a missing persons case. Given her propensity toward drugs and extramarital flings, different theories developed concerning her whereabouts. Police also found an eyewitness who spotted Gail at a bagel shop around 3 P.M., just after Robert said she left the apartment. But Gail's family had their own theory, and they pointed the finger at Robert. Aside from what they knew about the intimate and violent details of their marriage, Robert further infuriated Gail's family by coldly packing her personal items in trash bags. The family told police Gail didn't just vanish into thin air. She had been murdered. The police gravitated toward the same theory, but with no body and no evidence, the case vanished just as Gail had.

Robert moved to Las Vegas in 1989, remarried, and then moved to Minot, North Dakota, in 1995 with his second wife Janet and their infant daughter. More than a decade after Gail disappeared, a retiring prosecutor from the Manhattan district attorney's office decided to take one last look at the cold case files, and he noticed that Robert was a pilot.

He sent investigators to comb through logbooks at several New Jersey airports. It was at the Essex County airport that they found Robert took a two-hour flight, logged in on August 7, 1985. But the logbook had been changed from the day of the original flight, July 7, 1985. Police learned that Robert had rented a Cessna 172, which does not have autopilot but can be flown for short periods without holding on to the steering wheel once cruising altitude is reached.

Police quickly theorized that Robert had strangled Gail in their apartment, packed her body or body parts into his car, and driven to New Jersey, where he had taken off alone for two hours, during which time he had dumped Gail's remains over the Atlantic Ocean.

In December 1999, with no body and no physical evidence, Robert Bierenbaum was charged with the murder of his wife Gail. Nearly a year later, in the fall of 2000, armed only with circumstantial evidence, a jury convicted Robert of second-degree murder. He was sentenced to twenty-five years to life in prison.

FOR the Bierenbaums, theirs was a marriage destined for violence.

Gail was diagnosed by one therapist as having a condition called borderline personality disorder. Borderlines are notorious for having stormy relationships. First they love you, since you're the "all good one and savior," and then they hate you now that you're "all bad and the devil." Robert had been both to Gail.

It's not uncommon for people with this disorder to view themselves as bad and unworthy, which is why they often find themselves in abusive and dangerous relationships. They have no idea who they are and tend to feel misunderstood, mistreated, bored, and empty. These were common feelings for Gail. Borderlines' relationships with family are also stormy and tend to shift from feelings of idealization, great admiration, and love to intense anger, dislike, and devaluation within moments, and sometimes for no real reason at all. Gail's relationship with her family also fit this turbulent pattern. She had heated arguments with her parents prior to her marriage, but once she married, and her arguments and dissatisfaction were focused and projected onto her new husband, Robert, who had his own set of pathologies, it was a toxic mix.

There's no doubt that Gail admired her husband's intellect and goal-directedness. He embodied what she wanted to be. A part of her knew that if she chose Robert, she could be more like him professionally and strengthen her previously underdeveloped intellectual aspect. But even with this intellectual growth spurt, Gail couldn't help but stick it to her husband. She seemed to enjoy letting him know how much he was failing her.

People with borderline personality disorder exhibit plenty of rage and often can't stop themselves from discharging this rage onto the person who disappoints them. They have difficulty feeling soothed and okay with the world, and because of this they blame the person they are with since it seems to them that that person is the cause of their discomfort.

Robert became the unfortunate target of Gail's chronic and persistent upset and inability to feel good about herself. But he was the wrong guy to target these feelings onto; Gail's behavior enraged him, made him feel murderous and out of control. He had always been able to conquer the challenges that came his way. He could fly a plane, go to medical school, become a surgical resident, even cook and play the guitar. In his mind, there was very little he couldn't do, except win his wife's love and admiration. This, in turn, made him angry and resentful, and his anger toward Gail was becoming lethal.

Here is a case where you have two major character pathologies somehow finding each other—Gail was a suicidal and self-destructive borderline personality, Robert was an angry and violent perfectionist who wanted complete control, and he thought with increased intensity about killing Gail, leading to an incident when he tried to strangle her. Despite the violence, and the warning from a psychiatrist that Gail was in danger, she remained in the relationship. On some level the dangerous aspect of Robert's personality provided a macabre fascination for Gail. As uncomfortable as it was for her, it also made her feel excited and alive. Her anger toward her husband also gave her permission to have affairs with other men, argue with him, and do whatever else she wanted to do while married. What Gail didn't realize was that Robert's anger, and the subsequent violence, were his way of making himself whole.

Abusive husbands have an enormous need to feel good about themselves. When a man goes home to his wife he wants something to take place between the two of them that will help him to feel emotionally taken care of. The origins for this need lie in the mother/infant or young child relationship, with the mother serving as the central figure for this attachment style. The child has an enormous need to look into the eyes of his mother and see reflected back the messages "You make me happy" and "You are wonderful." All children, especially during their earliest development, require acknowledgment from their parents. This helps a child to feel pride and take pleasure in his or her accomplishments. When children are deprived of these essential responses, and instead are subjected to criticism for their efforts, they become emotionally stunted and may lose their innate ability to feel competent and confident.

Consequently, when they become adults these deprived children are always looking to someone in the outside world to validate and recognize them. The problem is, no mother—or any other person, for that matter—can be the perfect mirror. In some cases, there is a temperamental mismatch between parent and child, so that the child feels misunderstood, unappreciated, and out of sync with his primary caregiver. When this happens a child can develop a gap in his sense of self-worth and doubt his own self-competence. He then turns desperately to the outside world for validation and even more than most people, becomes excessively sensitized to signals that hint that he is unneeded, unsuccessful, and unappreciated.

Men, like women, depend on their partner to reassure them of their self-worth. When a woman does not offer this support, if his expectations are too high or if he feels she is deliberately withholding it, many men feel lost. Some respond by proving their virility with violence and taking control. When a woman is married to an abusive and overly controlling man, she gets blamed for not providing this important feedback the way, in his mind, she promised. Such men develop a hypersensitivity to the possibility of humiliation. To defend against feeling this dysphoric state, many men engage in controlling behavior, such as emotional, verbal, or physical abuse, to eliminate the source of discomfort and regain a sense of well-being.

Robert was more dependent on Gail than she realized, and when his needs were not met, he could not tolerate his unpleasant emotional response. He knew his wife wanted to leave him and was having affairs with other men. He did not so much want to control his wife as to make her stop making him suffer and feel bad. He needed her to think well of him in order to think well of himself. His violence toward her was an attempt to regain his sense of self. Batterers, like Robert, often feel that they are exploding within or coming apart when they are threatened. In the moment that they abuse, they do not know how to defend themselves against feelings of being demonized or dehumanized. Such men also tend to feel that their spouse is intentionally making them feel this way. So, on the outside the violence and controlling battering behavior are always secondary to the primary goal of protecting oneself psychologically.

Both Gail and Robert were notorious for blaming each other for their internal emotional states. The reality was that neither of them had the capacity to deal with their own internal mental discomfort. They both pointed the finger at each other instead of taking responsibility for their own behavior and looking to themselves to deal with their negative feelings. Robert and Gail gave each other good reasons to believe the other was the primary cause of their problematic emotional and marital state.

But Gail stepped over the line when she threatened Robert's professional existence. He had worked too long and too hard to have his career ended, especially by someone who brought on these murderous impulses with her infidelities and imperfections. He knew Gail wanted to leave him. But when she threatened to ruin his surgical career by publicizing the letter stating he was psychotic and violent, she had gone too far. Gail had embarked on an unconscious suicide mission. Just as she was on the brink of scholastic success and social independence, she pushed her husband way too far. Robert was enraged, and he was not going to let anyone or anything stop him from achieving a successful career.

Like many abusing and controlling men Robert felt his life being threatened and his internal experience, if he could describe it in words, would sound like this: "*What does she want from me? I can't take it anymore. She's unbearable and trying to make me feel like total garbage. She is going to ruin me, and she won't stop until she destroys me. I'm going to explode and become completely annihilated.*"

A surgeon has the power of life and death in his hands every day, and Robert was someone who, outside his home, was treated like a god and hero. But in someone like Robert, who has sociopathic tendencies and believes himself to be above the law, such godlike feelings can become lethal.

Robert's marriage and his career were about to end, and he decided to take matters into his hands once and for all. It was clear to him that Gail was never going to be the wife he needed her to be. She was too vituperative and rebellious. She was like a cancerous tumor in his life that needed to be surgically removed and discarded. Once this tumor was eliminated he could get on with his life. Besides, she made him do it, and furthermore she had been asking for this for a long time, with all the affairs, the complaining, the cruel and devaluing words. He had enough.

He knew from professional experience that you don't keep toxic tumors in your body. You get rid of them. Gail had become the toxic tumor in his life, so he terminated her.

Richard Sharpe also knew about toxic tumors.

A Harvard-trained dermatologist, Richard was a multimillionaire, having established a chain of hair removal clinics throughout Massachusetts. His fortune allowed Richard, a Mick Jagger look-alike, and his wife Karen, to easily navigate the Boston social scene, rubbing elbows with local celebrities and power brokers.

In turn, Richard and Karen were seen as a delightful couple. Everyone knew they were teenage sweethearts who married in 1973 soon after graduating from Shelton High School in Connecticut, and after Karen gave birth to a daughter, Shannon. They moved to Boston in 1985 so Richard could attend Harvard Medical School while Karen studied nursing. By 1995 Richard had a successful dermatology practice and founded his laser hair removal company, from which he would reap millions. The couple would have two more children, Michael and Alexandra, and settle into a colonial home in the suburbs, appearing to be the perfect family.

But behind the façade was a violent trail of abuse that went back more than two decades, ending only when Richard shot and killed his wife with a hunting rifle.

It was during the subsequent investigation and intense media coverage that Richard's friends, and the police, learned of his bizarre secrets, and of the incredible violence that overwhelmed his marriage. Richard was actually a cross-dresser who often beat his wife. After learning she had an affair in 1991, he stabbed her in the head with a fork, an incident which sent Karen to the hospital. Richard was subsequently committed to a mental facility and diagnosed as suffering from depression, anxiety, and personality disorders. Surprisingly, Karen later withdrew a police complaint and reconciled with her husband.

In actuality, the violence had begun early in their relationship, in the mid 1970s, and it escalated during the 1980s. During one car ride home following a New Year's Eve party, Richard beat Karen to a bloody pulp; she suffered a broken nose and a concussion. The couple tried to book a room at a motel but were turned away after the clerk saw Karen's bloodied face and clothing. On another occasion Karen alleged that her husband locked her inside their home for two days and abused her. When he took her to the hospital, he allegedly told his wife that he wanted her "to die."

It would seem, as Richard became more successful, his violent behavior escalated (Richard had reportedly even attempted to choke their daughter Shannon). He also grew more erratic. After opening his hair removal companies he used his facilities to erase his own body hair. And in an effort to grow breasts, he prescribed hormones for himself while ingesting his wife's birth control pills. He even wore his daughters' underwear, claiming it "fit" better than his wife's.

Karen never told a soul about her difficulties with her husband, not her family, friends, or neighbors. But by 2000 Karen took the children and left the home. She also obtained a restraining order against her husband of twenty-seven years. But that didn't help her on the night of July 14, 2000. Karen spent the evening out with friends and relatives, and soon after returning to her Wenham home the doorbell rang. It was Richard. Karen angrily told him he had to leave, holding up a copy of the restraining order. Richard ignored her, stepped into the foyer holding a hunting rifle, and fired a single shot into Karen's chest, killing her in front of her brother, a babysitter, and others. Richard ran from the home, but he was captured two days later in New Hampshire.

During his trial Richard admitted to killing his wife, but his lawyers argued that he was mentally incompetent and didn't know what he was doing. One defense psychiatrist testified that Richard was in such a "dissociative state" and out of contact with reality he wasn't able to function as himself. He regularly mixed numerous prescription drugs with alcohol and had suffered from various mental disorders. Richard himself claimed the evening of the murder was a "blur," and his intentions were to get his family together again but somehow he stole a gun and shot his wife. For what, he said he didn't know.

Prosecutors argued that Richard was far more clear-headed than he led the jury to believe, and that he killed his wife because she took $3 million from his account and was carrying on a love affair with a contractor. The jury also heard about Richard's interest in wearing wigs and women's clothing, including high heels and fishnet stockings.

But a defense psychiatrist said Richard's problems began long before there was any missing money. Richard, he said, suffered major depression and intermittent explosive disorder, which meant that he was unable to control sudden impulses, such as killing a spouse. The doctor added that Richard had suffered from abuse as a child at the hands of his own father. As a toddler he allegedly witnessed a beating in which his father had struck his brother on the head with a crowbar. According to the psychiatrist, Richard would dress in his sister's clothing in order to escape similar abuse. That sister, Lauri, was apparently his father's favorite child, said the psychiatrist, and not subject to the same abuse. So it was Richard's belief that if he dressed like his sister and looked like her, he'd escape the torture. The cross-dressing, said Richard, was a way to cope with the violence. With his early childhood such a mess, it would seem surprising that Richard would manage to marry at all. Yet he did, and Karen had brought normalcy to his life. Fearing the finality of losing her unglued him.

The prosecutors, of course, didn't buy any of it. They pointed to the hunting rifle, which Richard disposed of after killing his estranged wife, and his bid to flee. In the end, despite the dark tales of mental illness and bizarre cross-dressing, and Richard's plea of not guilty by reason of insanity, the jury believed Richard was sane enough the night he killed his wife and found him guilty of murder. He was sentenced to life in prison.

IF Richard Sharpe was a movie character he'd be Norman Bates, the deranged cross-dressing motel owner in Alfred Hitchcock's *Psycho.*

Richard had multiple problems compounded by years of drug abuse that clearly contributed to his deteriorating mental state. In addition to all of his other diagnoses, which included depression, anxiety, intermittent personality disorder, and sexual paraphilias, he was also a very paranoid guy. And paranoid men with shattered egos, like Richard Sharpe, don't do well in their relationships.

For Richard, his problems stemmed in large part from childhood abuse.

There is an accumulation of evidence to support that many spousal murderers witnessed violence in their childhood homes and/or were directly victimized by family members when they were children. Also, 40 percent of wife killers have witnessed a parent, usually a mother, being assaulted by a male partner.

According to researchers Angela Browne, Kirk Williams, and Donald Dutton, a link suggests that severe physical abuse and neglect during childhood makes a partner, particularly a male, vulnerable to using violence to resolve conflicts. Childhood abuse traumatizes a person's inner and outer experience to the point where it is both scarring and debilitating, and Richard was abused not only physically and emotionally, but forced to witness sexual abuse, which caused some gender confusion on his part.

It is well known that many abused children become abusers themselves. In the book *Intimate Violence,* Joseph Scalia, who works with batterers, compiles some interesting insights and ideas about this topic. For example, he notes that Anna Freud, daughter of Dr. Sigmund Freud and a well-known child psychoanalyst in her own right, wonders if adults who have been abused in childhood feel a sense of joy when they batter because it frees them from their own sense of victimhood. Anna Freud says by "impersonating the aggressor, assuming his attributes or imitating his aggression, the child transforms from the person threatened to the person who makes the threat." In other words, the person transforms himself from powerless into powerful, a major theme with abusive spouses.

Because these abusive personalities are unable to tolerate their own unpleasant emotional experiences by allowing themselves to re-experience the feeling of victimization, the batterers figuratively become their original victimizers. The abused child turns into an adult when he feels threatened and will do whatever it takes to preserve his sense of self and self-esteem. He really believes that the other person, in Dr. Sharpe's case his spouse, is trying to destroy him (at least in the moment). He feels that he is about to explode or disintegrate and become overloaded by his own emotions, and is then uncontrollable.

Drug and alcohol abuse also plays a role in partner abuse and femicide. Research shows that such addictions increase partner abuse eightfold and also contribute to femicide and attempted femicide twofold. One study revealed that men are more violent when killing their spouse than when killing any other known or unknown victim. There is an overkill quality to these kinds of killings, reflective of their emotional elements.

In effect, given his addictions, Richard had been disintegrating in a serious way for a very long time. The sociopathic aspect of his personality would also suggest that he felt he was above everything. He was out of control on multiple levels, and the motive to control was an attempt to feel safer and more protected. Paranoia thrives on ambiguity. And paranoids imagine the very worst in any scenario when the facts are unclear. They never really feel completely sure or completely safe about anything, which is very similar to how Richard felt during his youth. As an adult, there was something about the façade of being married that protected him and made him feel normal.

Along with his power and control issues, Richard also had signs of schizotypal personality disorder. People with this disorder tend to be suspicious of others and other people's motives. They often have unusual perceptual experiences, have virtually no close friends, and other people find their behavior or appearance to be odd.

Men like Richard are drawn to what gives them pleasure at the moment, which in his case was to be and feel like a woman. *I'll try on a dress. I wonder what it's like to get a period, so I'll try some hormones. I'm curious about what it's like to be a woman, so I'll grow some breasts.*

He was obviously confused about his gender identity, with a blurring of the lines between him and his wife. Thus, when Karen left, the mirage of a normal life was gone and in a true break in psyche, he lost his feminine side. And because his psyche was so disturbed, he believed that his wife was not, in fact, a separate person, but a part of himself. Being with Karen gave him a façade that prevented him from disintegrating further or becoming a full-fledged paranoid schizophrenic. With Karen's departure, however, the feminine part, his ideal, was gone too. And in order to keep that feminine side of himself, and to keep himself whole, he had to kill her. He knew there was a restraining order against him, and that he was not supposed to be anywhere near his wife on the night that he killed her. But he went regardless. He was fighting an instinctual struggle for survival. In his delusional mind, once Karen was dead, she'd stay linked with him forever.

4

The Sociopathic Killer

DURING the early part of the nineteenth century, psychopathology was considered a type of "moral insanity." One of the first clinicians, a French psychiatrist named Philippe Pinel, used the term "insanity without delirium" to describe the lack of restraint and complete remorselessness typical of sociopaths. The more common names for it today are "antisocial personality disorder" or "sociopathology."

The sociopath knows the difference between right and wrong, he just doesn't care about it. Instead he follows his own rules and laws. Although not all sociopaths are killers, their lack of feeling and tendency to devalue human life, along with their inclination to feel victimized and rejected, makes them much more inclined to consider murder as an option.

Sociopaths, in addition to engaging in purposeless and irrational behavior, also tend to be fearless thrill seekers. Punishment does not deter them because they are impulsive and bold in the face of consequences. They are also incapable of forming close or intimate relationships. People are just a means to an end. You're either someone who's useful to them or someone who's in the way. Sociopaths also have a grossly inflated view of themselves and tend to see themselves as the center of the universe. This is one reason they feel they should live by their own rules instead of the laws of the land. The sociopath can come across as self-assured, dominating, and arrogant. But he can also be glib, charming, and ingratiating.

Perhaps most disturbing is that sociopaths cannot be successfully treated because they are incapable of opening up to others, and, more important, they don't want to change. And what makes the sociopaths so dangerous is their amazing ability to rationalize outrageous behavior and dismiss personal responsibility for their actions.

TAKE, for example, CHRISTIAN LONGO.

Christian appeared to be just like any other tourist enjoying the warm sun and pristine beaches of Cancún, Mexico. He snorkeled during the day, danced at night, and found the intimate company of a German woman. He was, he told her, a writer.

Those who met him on trips to the Mayan ruins or group swims into spectacular underwater caverns thought Christian, twenty-eight, was wealthy. He was clean cut, handsome, and articulate, his easy smile and good humor entertaining all between sips of wine and puffs of marijuana. He appeared to have not a care in the world. It was only when police arrived on January 13, 2002, and surrounded the quaint village where Christian lived that those he befriended learned that he was a murderer, on the run from the FBI and Oregon authorities for killing his wife, Mary Jane, thirty-four, and three young children, Zachary, four,

Sadie Ann, three, and Madison, two. Their bodies were found just weeks earlier, in December, near Newport, Oregon. Madison had been strangled and stuffed into a dark green suitcase and tossed in Yaquina Bay, just behind the condominium where the family had lived. Sadie's body was found under nine feet of water with a pillowcase holding a large rock tied to her ankle. Zachary had been strangled and thrown into the bay. Mary Jane was also stuffed in a suitcase after having been strangled and beaten about the head.

For Christian, killing his wife and young children were the last desperate and heinous acts in a life filled with lies and deception.

Originally from Iowa, Christian Longo grew up in Michigan but left home when he was eighteen to pursue a relationship with Mary Jane, who was seven years older. They were both Jehovah's Witnesses, and they married in 1993 in Ann Arbor, Michigan, where they remained to work and raise a family. But just seven years later, broke and desperate, Christian and Mary Jane set out for Newport, Oregon, with their three children in tow. Unbeknownst to Mary Jane, her husband was also on the run from the law, having forged $30,000 worth of checks through his construction cleaning business. He had also defaulted on car leases, written bad checks on his own accounts, and maxed out his own and other people's credit cards. He was also being sued by various people and had been arrested for larceny for stealing a minivan from a dealer in Ohio. He took the vehicle under the guise of test-driving it, and when he drove it home he lied to his wife, claiming he had financed its purchase. Perhaps the greatest indignity came *following* his brushes with the law. Aware of the charges against Christian, the members of the Golfside Congregation of Jehovah's Witnesses asked him to leave.

On the way to Newport the Longos stopped in Portland to

pawn Mary Jane's wedding ring. But soon they were broke again and forced to live in cheap motels while eating only bread and ramen noodles. Three months later, they were living in an upscale condominium complex after Christian convinced the condo manager that he worked for a communications company and would pay the first month's $1,200 rent when his check arrived. In reality at the time he was earning only $1,200 a month clerking in a variety store and a coffee shop.

Following his capture in Mexico, Christian explained to police that by mid-December there was no money and no food and he was at his wits' end, unable to care for his family.

During the subsequent trial, prosecutors painted Christian as a man who tired of his family, which prevented him from living a flamboyant lifestyle. They said that after he killed his wife and children the morning of December 17, Christian was spotted near a bridge that spanned the bay. Later that morning he had coffee at a Starbucks and returned rented movies to a video store. The following day employees at an inn where the family had once stayed found all of the Longo family belongings, including baby clothes, women's clothing, family photos, and Mary Jane Longo's Michigan identification, in a trash bin. That night Christian attended a holiday party at a pizza parlor for employees of a local Starbucks where he had once worked. He told a coworker that his family had moved back to Michigan and would not return.

On December 19 Christian's maroon minivan was found at a local auto dealership. Inside were toys and other items, including a book titled *Running from the Law.* Over by the bay behind the condominium where they had lived, the body of his son, Zachary, was discovered floating facedown. Three days later Sadie's body was recovered from the water. Both children had been drowned. It would be another week before police recovered the bodies of Madison and Mary Jane.

By then Christian had driven to San Francisco in a stolen car, stayed two nights at a youth hostel, then boarded a flight to Mexico using identification he had stolen in Oregon.

For his part Christian blamed the murders on Mary Jane, whom he said became hysterical after he confessed to his lies and infidelities. Mary Jane, described by those who knew her as a loving wife and doting mother, killed the two oldest children, said Christian, who claimed he became enraged and retaliated by grabbing Mary Jane around the neck and lifting her up off the floor. He then claimed he turned his anger on his youngest daughter.

Christian's defense, and overall demeanor during the trial, infuriated all. In their closing arguments prosecutors labeled Christian an egotistical liar who killed his family so that he could begin anew.

The jury took little time in delivering a guilty verdict and sentencing Christian to death.

WITH his good looks and charming personality, Christian Longo is probably the most evil and scary of the intimate-partner killers reported on in this book.

Like a true sociopath, Christian Longo focused on expedience and living in the moment. He was unable to resist a good opportunity, even if seizing it meant breaking the law. For this kind of personality, violence and threats are just handy strategies to use when they are angered, defied, or frustrated. They give little thought to the pain and degradation they impose on their victims, in part because they don't really care. They will do whatever it takes to satisfy their own needs.

Unlike a normal person, who can empathize and understand another person's emotional experience, the sociopath cannot. They know they are not like other people. They don't think that other people have valid opinions different from their own and they react to others with indifference, a feeling of power, pleasure, and/or a smug satisfaction. They are not going to lose any sleep over what they have done because they don't think they have done anything wrong, even if they have committed murder.

Like Christian Longo's their violent crimes are callous and cold-blooded. As opposed to killers who kill because they are in an intense emotional state, classic sociopaths kill for an entirely different reason. They don't kill because they are necessarily distressed or for the more "logical" precipitating factors such as jealousy or rage. Instead they kill in a straightforward, often businesslike and uncomplicated way. Sometimes they even see themselves as the true victims and are able to rationalize their behavior, which helps them to dismiss personal responsibility for their actions. They can even tell themselves that their crimes had a positive impact on their victims.

Christian Longo, like many sociopaths, was extraordinarily glib and charming. With his blond hair and all-American good looks he appeared to be the epitome of refinement. He had a natural ability to make a good impression. Even his father-in-law, Jim Baker, remembered being very impressed by him, even though Christian was seven years younger than his daughter, Mary Jane. During the early years of their relationship, Baker described him as being very together, well dressed, with an engaging and mature personality. Longo seemed to have it all over the other young men his age.

Christian and Mary Jane met through their church. Both were Jehovah's Witnesses. She was shy and naïve and had a very sheltered upbringing, living with her mother right up until the day of her wedding. Mary Jane was definitely no match for her husband's devious and sinister ways. She was a good person and a good wife who worked while her husband bounced from job to job. They had three children in a relatively short period of time and they were always impeccably dressed and lovely to be around. As much as Mary Jane tried to keep things together, Christian's devious character surfaced quickly and made it difficult to maintain a stable family life.

Christian saw love as a game and the people in his life as pawns in that game. In Mary Jane he chose a woman he could easily manipulate and deceive, knowing she'd never question him or tell him what to do. She knew her place in a relationship, which is what drew Christian toward her. Christian was also an expert at hiding bad intentions behind a sophisticated and well-spoken façade. No one was better at looking good than he was, always emitting the impression that he was Mr. Right (even though he clearly turned out to be Mr. Wrong). For Christian, "love" was just a means to an end. It helped him to exploit his future victims. Words were used as tools and weapons to sway, swindle, and get one over on people.

Christian was a genius at creating psychological chaos in the people who were close to him. That was becoming an all too clear reality for his family, especially for Mary Jane. The Longos would soon be on the run. They were running away from all the problems and difficulties Christian created along the way. Many close to Mary Jane believed she was either too scared to leave or did not really understand the magnitude of what was going on. When her sisters told her they were concerned about her and her children's welfare, she emphatically denied that there were any problems in her marriage.

Christian's gypsy life may have been the first sign of his soon to be murderous desperation. Despite his instability Christian, in keeping with his sociopathic demeanor, could be outgoing, verbally proficient, and charming even under the worst of circumstances. Sociopaths typically are calm and collected. It's not hard for them to appear like everything is under control.

Their ties to family are slender at best and they have no need to give or receive love, an emotion that has no real meaning for them. They have no desire to maintain any type of familial connection, and they suffer from an emotional poverty that interferes with their ability to have a wide range of feelings—yet another of the qualities that makes this type so dangerous.

People with antisocial personality tendencies have decreased levels of arousal. This can lead them to indulge in sensation-seeking behaviors, and can also engender a greater desire to experience stimulating events. Christian had tried out the role of religious family man with his wife and three kids, but it didn't work. Living in dingy hotels with barely any money for food was slowing him down too. It was a drag. And once what little money he did have ran out, Christian's murderous tendencies took over. The need to feel superior mattered more to him than his family's welfare and he knew he needed to make a change, and make it fast. Unfortunately for his family, Christian's needs came first. He just didn't care much about people and was incapable of loyalty or guilt. He never really had any lasting relationships in his life, but he thought things would be different when he had a family of his own. It seemed to work for other people, who appeared to love and feel connected to their families. It was a worthwhile experiment, but Christian soon realized that it was an experiment that had failed since nothing really changed for him. In fact, having a family made things much worse.

He was attracted to Mary Jane when they first met, and he even enjoyed her physical comfort and the material and emotional support she once offered him. But things changed. It was time for a new role, and a new life; one where he could move around alone in a way family life would never allow him to do. He longed for a new kind of freedom and an unencumbered lifestyle. It wasn't that he hated Mary Jane or the kids, not at all. The problem is he really did not feel anything toward them. In his mind, since he had created them, he should be able to eliminate them. Like the clothes and the family photos he threw in the trash, his family was no longer convenient to him and so had to be dismissed.

Following his unbelievable acts of human cruelty, Christian completely redefined his life by moving to Mexico. He found himself a girlfriend, passed himself off as a successful travel writer, and enjoyed drinking and snorkeling with some new foreign acquaintances. *This was more like it.* It was the vacation and lifestyle he was born to have. He deserved it! He should have realized this before! He resented all the responsibilities and pressures that having a wife and kids placed on him. *Note to self: Not having a family is a good thing.* He justified his actions, believing that his murdered family members were probably in a better place anyway. They were good Christians. They should be in heaven right now. He now was more confident than ever that Mary Jane and the kids were obstacles to happiness, and that was simply not allowed. He was finally happy. How could that be wrong?

In the real world familicide is the killing of one's entire family and there are several different reasons for this aberrant behavior. Some of the motivations that apply to the Longo case include losing control of family circumstances, not wanting to feel powerless, seeing only adverse circumstances ahead in life if the family was not killed off, in addition to seeing the deaths as a necessary sacrifice. There is also a sense of ownership/entitlement and possessiveness about murder, based on a tremendous difficulty adjusting to parenthood, and a belief that the role of a wife and child/children is to satisfy one's own personal needs.

The bottom line was Christian Longo thought no life was more important or meaningful than his own. The hostility required to take the life of one's own wife and children before discarding them and everything they own is unimaginable to most of us, but it is also a clear sign of extreme revulsion and disregard for the human condition.

WHILE Christian Longo killed to free himself into a dream world, MARK HACKING created a fantasy world he couldn't escape.

For Mark and his wife Lori Soares, their lives together finally appeared to come into focus. Lori, twenty-seven, had just learned she was five weeks pregnant. And the couple was preparing to move cross-country from their home in Utah to North Carolina, where Mark, a health care assistant, had enrolled in the University of North Carolina medical school. With her first child on the way, and a future filled with so much promise, there was much to look forward to for the Hackings.

But on Friday, July 16, 2004, Lori, a trading assistant at Wells Fargo, left work early, visibly upset. She had just called the University of North Carolina inquiring about financial aid for her husband but was told that he had never enrolled there and had never even applied. When she confronted him that evening, Mark claimed it must be a computer glitch. Two days later, he told her the shocking truth: He never enrolled in medical school, and had never even graduated from the University of Utah. For Lori, it was the last straw in a marriage filled with too many lies and deceptions.

After Mark delivered the crushing news about his education and medical school, Lori went to bed that Sunday night sure that her marriage was over. She had even written a letter telling him that she no longer saw any future for them. Later that night, around 1 A.M., after several hours playing video games, Mark quietly walked into the bedroom and pointed a .22 rifle at Lori's head. He fired a single shot, killing his sleeping wife. The next morning he called Lori's office, and then her friends and family, saying she went jogging around 5:30 A.M. and never returned. A massive search ensued and the heartfelt pleas from Lori's family were broadcast throughout the region and the nation, begging for her safe return. As police began their investigation, Mark checked himself into a psychiatric ward after suffering a mental breakdown, the emotional toll apparently too much to bear. In reality, it was the police who were bearing down on Mark.

The day he reported her missing, police searched their apartment and found a bloody knife, a receipt for a new mattress, and Lori's letter. The knife, theorized police, was used to carve the mattress, which was later found, bloodied and cut up, in a trash bin near the University of Utah, where Mark worked. The receipt indicated Mark had bought the new mattress less than an hour before he made his first call inquiring as to Lori's whereabouts. When they inspected Lori's car, which was recovered near the jogging trail, the police found that the seat had been adjusted to fit someone larger than Lori. They also found the keys to the car inside the Hacking apartment. As they collected their overwhelming evidence, it became clear who had killed Lori Hacking.

On July 24, just five days after she disappeared, Mark gave up his last deception, disclosing the awful truth about the fate of his pregnant wife to his brothers Lance and Scott. Mark told them that after killing Lori, he wrapped her body with garbage bags and placed it in a Dumpster. He then took the bloody mattress, cut it to pieces, and placed it in a trash bin near a church. He also took Lori's car and parked it near the jogging trail, and then visited a local furniture store and purchased the new mattress. Believing he had covered his tracks, Mark called Lori's office, inquiring as to her whereabouts.

Upon his release from the mental facility, and following his confession to his brothers, Mark was arrested and charged with Lori's murder. Two months later Lori's body was found in a landfill, identifiable only through dental records. In April 2005, Mark pled guilty to killing his wife and was sentenced to sixty years life in prison.

THE murder and subsequent cover-up were all too shocking for the conservative state capital of Salt Lake City. The Hackings had been together there for ten years, and their relationship appeared to be strong, with Lori, a pretty, private, reserved woman, calling her husband a "teddy bear." In return Mark, an outgoing man who enjoyed joking around, even at his own expense, was said to have adored his wife.

But the first seeds of doubt were planted in 2002 when, unknown to anyone at the time, Mark secretly dropped out of the University of Utah after three years of study. Lori learned about this only after Mark's mother called to say she could not pay his tuition because he was not enrolled. Mark said that he simply forgot to register. The couple reconciled and Mark returned to school. Or so everyone thought. A year later he began his supposed preparations for medical school. But this deception was far more elaborate than his previous ones. At one point he traveled to New York under the guise that he was interviewing for medical school there. He stayed with a cousin and on the day of the "interview" he dressed in a suit. Upon his return several hours later he discussed the "interview" in depth.

Previously Lori thought that her husband had received his bachelor's degree and was set to study medicine in North Carolina. Now disabused of that notion and pregnant, her long-time dreams to become a mother and to have her own family shattered, Lori needed time to decide her future. But only a few hours later, Mark made that decision for her. It was the end of a union that had at first thrilled both families.

The Hackings loved Lori and the Soares family loved

Mark. Especially Thelma, Lori's mother. To her, Mark was more like a son than a son-in-law, which made her daughter's murder even more devastating. And like many such murders, no one ever saw it coming.

Mark was born into a very accomplished family. His father was a well-known and well-respected pediatrician. His brothers were also professionals, one a doctor and the other an engineer. Mark told everyone he was going to follow in his family's footsteps, his sights set on becoming a doctor. Everyone believed him and supported his dream. No one had any reason not to.

Mark and Lori were known by their friends and family to have a wonderful relationship. She was the more practical of the two, he the more carefree and spontaneous, "goofy" and "fun loving" by nature. They seemed to be in perfect balance.

Mark, like many sociopaths, could be extremely charming and impressive. The classic sociopath is someone who habitually and disobeys social norms and fails to learn from past mistakes. Mark exhibited the more neurotic variety of sociopathy, in his case triggered by an intense lack of self-esteem and self-regard. To compensate for his deficiencies, he lied, and his lying was pathological. He simply could not stop himself since lying was an easy way for him to feel good about himself.

Even when Mark achieved some success, he never really believed that he was worth very much. But the people around him would never have guessed this about him. He covered it up by being the life of the party and enjoying conversations about medicine and his professional aspirations. He spoke with certainty about becoming a doctor. All of the unpleasant realities of his life, such as failing to graduate from college and never applying to or getting into medical school, had disappeared. It was like magic. The more that Mark could convince others about his lies, the more he convinced himself. It was as if he were on stage and the role of the successful Mark Hacking would be played today by the real and unsuccessful Mark Hacking. And the more he could convince others of his lies the worse they got, until they took on a powerful life of their own.

Even though Mark was not as successful as the other men in his family, this didn't mean that he didn't have a need to be admired and respected by those around him. In fact, this disparity in achievement increased his need for validation from others, especially his wife. So like other pathological lying sociopaths, Mark had a need to be the center of attention and to have people feel good about him. Since he was incapable of meeting life as it really was, he wove a mass of fantastic tales to help him cope, and lying became the way in which he could be the person he wanted to be. By lying Mark was able to reconstruct reality and make life the way it really should be.

People usually lie to make themselves look and feel better. Emotionally they have something to gain. They use lying as a tool to help improve their self-image and to decorate their personality, thus "becoming" who they really want to be, which allows them to say something or be someone who is interesting. In Mark's case, the lie became his real identity and thus became more important than the truth that Mark was trying to deny. Mark was sometimes all too aware of his chronic, persistent, and opposing feelings of desire and dissatisfaction. When pathological liars are so deep in their lies, they can often convince themselves that their version of the truth *is* the truth. When that happens, the lie becomes more like a wish psychosis, and the pathological liar presents himself as charming, enthusiastic, cheerful, free, and open. This is because he often believes his stories, at least while he is telling them. He wants the lie to be the truth, so in an odd way it is. Convincing others of his story helps him to convince himself.

Chronic liars such as Mark fall in love with themselves and are thrilled by their creative tales in much the same way that a novelist takes pleasure in a newly invented and creative plot. The liar's anecdotes serve two main purposes: impressing others and boosting the liar's self-image and self-esteem. In the psychological world this is called securing one's narcissistic supply. The stories always make liars feel more like who they want to be. The disturbed habit of lying stems from a need for acceptance, self-affirmation, and self-protection. Common motives for lying include a desire to stand out, to be more interesting, to win the adoration and respect of others, to eliminate personal feelings of failure, and to help the liar overcome the fear of not living up to other people's expectations. Perhaps most important, many liars feel like they are really imposters.

Pathological lying, or pseudologica fantastica, is a common feature in people with antisocial personality disorders. Clinical features of this disorder include a failure to conform to norms, deceitfulness, manipulativeness, impulsivity, failure to plan ahead, irritability, aggressiveness, reckless disregard for the safety of others, consistent irresponsibility, and a lack of remorse after having hurt, mistreated, or stolen from another person.

Some of the personality traits include a sense of entitlement, apathy toward others, unconscionable behavior, and being manipulative and cunning, socially irresponsible, disregardful of obligations, and nonconforming to social norms. As children compulsive liars tend to have little tolerance for criticism, and it is impossible to tell from their body language whether they are telling the truth or not. On the positive side, they tend to have better perceptions than the average person, better oral and written fluency, and have a gifted imagination. They also tend to have a knack for lying about things that they really do have a talent or knack for. The lying tends to start early in life during their formative years. They are often very dramatic, romantic, and glib talkers. This personality disorder reveals itself when the individual takes the path of least resistance. His moral weakness stops him from feeling any concern or empathy for others. The con artist type of liar, like Mark Hacking, exudes a self-confidence and spin webs of deception that can be very intriguing to others. Underneath the charm is often a cleverly masked but intense hostility.

Mark discovered early on he was only as lovable as his achievements. If he did not achieve, he did not feel loved. He was traumatized, and in his case it was especially depressing and enraging to have two brothers who were so successful. This made it even more difficult to compete. Sometimes you can be born into a perfectly "nice family," but because of your temperament, position, and some of the subtle messages between family members, an unhealthy psychological environment can be created. Mark felt enraged that he could not succeed, as had all the other men in his family.

The competitive nature of Mark's family contributed to his self-loathing and depression, and to deal with the competition he began to lie. And it was so easy to lie. This was the only time that he really felt in control as he transformed from the loser Mark Hacking into the winner Mark Hacking.

Like most sociopathic con artists, Mark knew intuitively what his family wanted and expected of him. His way to please them and win their affections was to become a master psychological illusionist. He was able to convince most people of almost anything. Meeting and falling in love with Lori only enhanced his feeling that he was special. He felt like he could do and be anything when he was around her. For her part, Lori knew that Mark had an irresponsible side, but he was always able to keep it in check. She had never met anyone like him. Even during their most intense and difficult times, he had a way of calming her down and making everything feel all right. What Lori didn't know was that Mark needed her to go along with his false image of himself in order to remain a nonviolent husband. If she could not go along with his lies about his identity, she would be in trouble. He needed this support from her on an unconscious level, yet resented it at the same time. The lying was his creation, and it took a lot of energy to make himself seem interesting, accomplished, and attractive.

As Mark's life spun out of control he had no one to confide in. When Lori had caught him in some small lies, he had been able to talk his way out. But as his lies grew, Mark knew he would have problems explaining himself if caught. And he had other problems on the horizon, most notably Lori's pregnancy. How was he going to manage being a father? He knew they could not make it on his small salary and that Lori needed to work in order to support the family. This new component only served to complicate his life even more. Lori also seemed less affectionate and loving, with the pregnancy making her more serious and irritable. Mark found her to be more demanding at home. A wife's pregnancy can make some men feel more aggressive, and Mark was falling into this category. The faux medical school, the move, the pregnancy—the pressure was becoming unbearable. The timing of all this could not be worse.

As the pressure increased and the lies were revealed, Lori was at her wits' end, and her confronting Mark left him paralyzed. He had been lying for so long it had become a necessary part of his psychic life. Without it, he really did not know how to function or how to survive or even who he was. As long as his lies were supported, he could operate "normally." As soon as they were confronted, he could not tolerate it psychologically, and he became enraged. Lori was supposed to be different from everyone else in his life, but she wasn't. She obviously could not love him for who he "really" was. Furthermore, he could not risk anyone else finding out about his situation. Everyone thought he was going to medical school to become a doctor, and Lori crossed a line when she told him he was a liar and a fake and that she was going to tell everyone. He would be exposed, and it made him feel vulnerable, victimized, and threatened. With his anger came the rationale that it was her fault that he felt humiliated. Maybe she did not need him anymore now that she was going to have a baby. He was useless; nothing more than a sperm donor. Now that she got what she wanted, she could leave him, thus spoiling his dream and his professional aspirations. For that, she had to be eliminated. If she was eliminated he could continue to live the way he always had lived. It was really the only way out for him.

I had an opportunity to meet Lori's mother, Thelma, during an *Oprah* program we did together. She is one of the loveliest people I have ever met. Still in pain over the loss of her daughter, she was trying to reconcile the two different Marks: the Mark that she loved and the Mark who lied and ultimately killed her daughter.

It was impossible for her to understand why he did not just walk away. She recalled how Mark's family blamed his problems on an accident that left him with a brain seizure. The medical information does not support this theory in causing his murderous behaviors. In reality, Mark Hacking had two sides. There was always an invisible screen separating him from others, a barrier he would find impossible to cross. He was left with two contradictory views of himself, one of his being superior and one of being inferior. Most of the time he lived in his head as he choreographed his own autobiography. The life he created through his lies was so much more exciting than the life he was actually living. His reality was not as enjoyable as his wished-for reality. It sustained him, and he could not live without it. It was like his antidepressant or antipsychotic medication. It was lifesaving and solved the conflict between himself and the world. What can compete with this kind of fantasy world?

Mark made himself heroic and his world dramatic. His friendly façade brilliantly masked his deep antagonism and hostility that even he feared. When he was playing the role of the successful Mark Hacking, all of his destructive urges and fiery aggression disappeared. His bitterness and fury rightfully frightened him. His fake life protected and relieved him from the intolerable pain he felt about his failure to live up to his own and other people's standards.

When Lori took this coping or defense mechanism away from him, there was nothing to stop his rage, his anger, and his diminished self-esteem. She had hit his Achilles' heel, the most vulnerable place in his psychic armor. He had thought love would stop his pain, not make it worse. He was pushed over the edge in a way that he never would have predicted. Lying was the only way he knew how to live in the world. He was not going to let Lori or anyone else take that away from him. If that meant murder, then so be it.

5

The Black Widow/Profit Killer

THE Black Widow Killer was named after the Latrodectus, a venomous and deadly spider that bites fast and hard and comes out of nowhere to mercilessly kill its victims. The Black Widow Killer is a woman who systematically murders a single or multiple spouses, partners, other family members, or individuals outside of the family with whom she has developed a personal and usually intimate relationship. However, the Black Widow overwhelmingly prefers to kill a trusted spouse or intimate partner.

This type of killer typically begins her criminal career after the age of twenty-five and may go on actively killing victims for a period of ten years and/or until she gets caught. Unlike Hollywood's glamorized portrayal of these women, such as Sharon Stone in *Basic Instinct* or Theresa Russell in *Black Widow,* they are not particularly glamorous or beautiful. In reality they tend to be more "Plain Jane–ish," which makes their diabolical abilities particularly intriguing to the outside world. The typical

American Black Widow relies on her ability to win the confidence and trust of those whom she will ultimately murder, with gaining that trust an essential prerequisite to her attacks. The Black Widow's perceived role as confidante to her eventual victims often provides her with the perfect alibi, and she is able to attack her victims with great precision. Poison is often her lethal weapon of choice; the death is slow and usually requires a long period of time.

This type of murderer usually has only one motive: profit. She tends to murder for life insurance proceeds or to receive her victim's financial assets. On rare occasions, rage and revenge also factor into her motive. She has an insatiable appetite for money; no amount is ever enough. When she needs more cash, her murderous impulses strike again, usually in a quiet, careful, and often undetected manner.

SUCH was the case of JULIA LYNN TURNER.

In March 1995, Maurice Glenn Turner, a Cobb County, Georgia, police officer, was taken to the emergency room at a local hospital, suffering from flulike symptoms. He was treated and released. The next day, Glenn, thirty-one, died. His death, said the coroner, was the result of an enlarged heart.

The day after Glenn's funeral his wife, Lynn (as she was known), called her husband's insurance company to put in a claim for benefits. As his sole beneficiary she was entitled to $110,000. She also received nearly $50,000 in employee benefits and a monthly pension check of nearly $800. Less than a week after her husband's death, Lynn, thirty, rented a new apartment with another man, Randy Thompson, a firefighter. The couple had been romantically involved, though Randy was unaware that Lynn was married. Following Glenn's death the couple even took a vacation to the Caribbean, with Lynn paying the bill with her insurance money.

Lynn and Randy lived together for the next four years, their relationship producing two children before ending amicably in 1998. They remained intimate, and in January 2001, Randy, then thirty-one, visited the emergency room complaining of flu-like symptoms following a dinner date with Lynn. He died shortly after his visit to the hospital, the cause of death initially determined to be heart failure. Lynn again applied for death benefits and this time received $36,000, which she used to clear up her credit cards and charges for thirty-three bounced checks. Several months later the mothers of Glenn Turner and Randy Thompson traded letters. They couldn't help but take notice that their sons had died after suffering similar symptoms, and both had been involved with Lynn. Their concerns reached the Georgia Bureau of Investigation, which opened an investigation focusing first on Randy Thompson, whose tissues were examined and found to contain calcium oxalate crystals, which could only have come from ethylene glycol poisoning. Ethylene glycol is found in antifreeze and even small doses can kill a person in a short period of time.

Investigators then exhumed Glenn Turner's body, six years after his death. He, too, had calcium oxalate crystals in his system. Investigators reviewed the police file on his death and saw two things that piqued their interest: a photo from the Turners' basement of a gasoline can and a bottle of antifreeze, and Lynn's statement that she gave her husband Jell-O several hours before he died. Investigators also learned that Glenn was contemplating a divorce.

The couple had married in August 1993 near Atlanta. Lynn had once worked in the district attorney's office and was a 911 operator when they met. Within a week after exchanging wedding vows Lynn demanded that Glenn make changes in his life insurance policy, which had listed his mother as beneficiary. Lynn wanted to be the beneficiary, and Glenn made the change, telling his insurance agent that his new wife was pressing him hard. Less than a year later the marriage had already hit rock bottom. Glenn and Lynn slept in separate beds, and her spending habits were so out of control Glenn had to take on an extra job for $7 an hour in order to pay their bills. While Glenn was trying to make ends meet, Lynn would go away every weekend. Glenn didn't know that his wife was involved in a torrid affair with Randy Thompson. He confided to a friend about the sorry state of his relationship with Lynn and said if things didn't improve he was going to file for divorce but that he first planned to talk to Lynn. A week later he was dead.

Police interviews with friends and family recalled how Lynn remained unemotional throughout Glenn's funeral, and how she didn't want her name in her husband's obituary. While everyone knew her as Lynn she wanted her real name, Julia, used in the notice. Several days later she moved in with Randy, and six years later Randy was dead. His friends and family, like those of Glenn Turner, told investigators there were few, if any, tears from Lynn during his funeral.

Police eventually arrested Lynn and charged her with murdering Glenn Turner, alleging that she had poisoned her husband by placing ethylene glycol in his Jell-O. During her trial in 2004 witnesses told of how she visited the local animal shelter inquiring about euthanizing cats and dogs, and experts on ethylene glycol poisoning told of their belief that Lynn gave her husband small doses, first to make him ill, then eventually to kill him. The judge also allowed testimony relating to the death of Randy Thompson, and experts said he, too, died from small doses of the same poison. It was a second dose given to him following his return from the hospital that killed him, they said. The jury found Lynn guilty of "malice murder," and she was sentenced to life in prison. In late 2004 she was indicted and charged with murdering Randy Thompson.

Her motivation in both murders, said prosecutors, was the insurance money.

• • •

According to Wilson and Daly, when it comes to intimate-partner murders, women commit seven murders for every ten committed by men. In some cities, such as Detroit, women killed more intimate partners by a 2 to 1 margin. And females who kill are documented as killing family members more often than they commit any other type of murder. In some cases there is a history of abuse within the household. In others infidelity is the cause. For the Black Widow, it's all about the money.

Emotions such as empathy, caring, remorse, and sympathy are absent in such women, especially those with a history of abuse. They suffer from an inability to feel connected to an environment that once made them feel safe and secure: But they are generally very intelligent; they will study the effects of and reactions to toxic substances for hours and search for ways to have poisons mimic other types of diagnosable illnesses. Sometimes the Black Widow will rely on specific agents she knows her husband or partner is violently allergic to, such as nuts, bee stings, or shellfish, in order to cause his untimely death.

Traditionally, Black Widows meet their husbands through widows' or widowers' clubs, lonely-hearts ads, or mutual acquaintances. It is not uncommon to successfully kill off one spouse, collect his money, and then move to a new location. The Black Widow's façade tends to hold up well, at least initially, partly because our society places so much faith in the notion of the trustworthy, faithful wife and mother. To think anything else about women and womanhood is too disturbing. The Black Widow knows this and deliberately targets those who are likely to trust her the most.

Glenn Turner knew his wife did not care for him. She even told him so during a heated argument, saying that she had never loved him. That was in marked contrast to what she claimed at the beginning of their relationship, when Lynn seduced Glenn with expensive gifts. It was after they married that friends saw subtle signs that something was amiss. During Lynn's trial they testified that she was seen reading a *Physicians' Desk Reference,* saying she was "interested in medicine and how the body worked." And at Glenn's funeral she infuriated everyone by wearing a hot-pink suit; her demeanor was cold and icy and she failed to shed any tears.

Lynn thought things would be different the second time around with Randy Thompson. Unlike Glenn, who she believed to be nothing but a wimp, and an easy target to kill, things were different with Randy. She loved him and wanted to spend the rest of her life with him. They even had two beautiful children together. But just like all the other men in her life, Randy eventually disappointed her.

Lynn had an aberrant form of OCD, otherwise known as obsessive compulsive disorder, which was evident in the perfectionist quality of her murders. She did the same thing in precisely the same way to both men. She saw both men in an emotionally detached way, used the same poison, and killed both for greed. She was like a little kid who sets up her blocks in the same way, repeating the pattern over and over and over again. Once Lynn entered into a relationship with each man, whatever distinct characteristics he possessed were lost. One was no different from the other—each was just a means to an end. For Lynn, they were nothing more than walking and talking ATM machines. And even though her motive seemed to be financial and centered on survival, she experienced a perverse satisfaction in the destruction of both of these men.

At her core, Lynn functioned like a woman who was abandoned, either physically or emotionally, by her father. One thing that is interesting about Lynn is that she did not target the Donald Trumps of her world. She did not pursue high earners such as doctors, lawyers, or investment bankers. Instead, she set her sights on lower-profile men, one a police officer and the other a firefighter. Unconsciously she sought the type of men she thought could both protect and demean her, a pair of behaviors she was used to. With both men she initially tried to be the "good enough girlfriend." She bought them gifts, which is the way some women believe they are supposed to behave if they want to win the prize. And Lynn was always good at getting her prize. When she killed the two men, there was a childlike/immature and repetitive quality about her crimes.

Killing became a compulsion, driven by an unconscious need to get caught. Lynn realized that once you step over that line, especially when it is so darn easy, it is really hard not to do it again. The successful crime leaves a neurological imprint in the brain. The route is already established to relieving tension in this way, so the next time there is tension it becomes harder to resist taking murderous action. It is as if a person is on autopilot.

That is exactly how Lynn felt the second time around—like she was on autopilot. The truth of the matter is, for Lynn, neither of these men treated her properly. Neither one knew how to take care of her emotionally or financially. Was killing them so wrong? Maybe the next time around she would get it right.

FOR KIMBERLY HRICKO, getting it right meant setting in motion her plan for murder.

On February 14, 1998, Kimberly and her husband Stephen arrived at the Harbourtowne resort in eastern Maryland for a Valentine's weekend getaway. They had been married for nine years but, like many couples, had drifted apart—in fact Kimberly, thirty-two, wanted a divorce. Her husband, she said, had become distant and cold, and whatever passion they once had between them had long vanished. But Stephen, thirty-five, wanted a second chance and suggested a romantic weekend away, which he believed would revive long-lost feelings. Kimberly agreed, and after arriving to a champagne greeting at the deluxe resort they later enjoyed a dinner theater presentation of a murder mystery called *The Bride Who Cried.*

Following dinner they returned to their cottage around 10:30 P.M., but two hours later Kimberly calmly walked into the lobby to tell the clerk that her room was on fire. Several employees ran to the cottage, which was filled with smoke. Inside was Stephen, lying in his pajamas between the twin beds, his upper torso and head badly charred. He was dead.

Kimberly told state police investigators that following dinner, Stephen, who had already drunk a bottle of champagne, picked up four bottles of beer before they returned to their cottage. They watched a movie together but then argued when Stephen pressed her for sex. Kimberly said, as part of their plan to resolve their differences, they had vowed not to be intimate during their "getting reacquainted" weekend. But Stephen had sought intimacy anyway, and Kimberly took the car keys and left the cottage, driving to visit their best friends, who lived fifteen minutes away. Kimberly said she couldn't find the house, got lost, and drove around for two hours before returning to the cottage, only to find it on fire and filled with smoke.

The subsequent autopsy on Stephen's body produced several unsettling results, most important the actual cause of his death. Despite the smoke and fire, there was no carbon monoxide in his lungs, which ruled out smoke inhalation. The toxicology report also indicated that his blood-alcohol level was 0.0, which meant he hadn't had a drink that night. It appeared that Stephen was already dead before the fire started. He had been poisoned, most likely by some yet-to-be-determined drug.

All eyes turned toward Kimberly.

The couple had met in State College, Pennsylvania, where Stephen was a student at Penn State University and Kimberly worked as a waitress. Stephen was instantly smitten, and following an intense courtship they married in March 1989. They eventually settled in Laurel, Maryland, where Stephen worked as a golf course superintendent and Kimberly became a certified surgical technologist, assisting with operations. One of her responsibilities was removing and disposing of all unused drugs following an operation.

The couple had a child, but several years into the marriage investigators learned that Kimberly became restless, complaining to friends that her husband was uncommunicative and unemotional. Her growing discontent led to a heated affair with a twenty-three-year-old man, the cousin of one of her friends. The affair began in December 1997, just two months before Stephen died. Prior to leaving for the weekend getaway with her husband, Kimberly left her boyfriend a Valentine's package and card proclaiming her love.

In the weeks before the deadly trip, Kimberly had made several shocking admissions, telling one friend she was involved with another man and telling others that she wished her husband were dead. When friends suggested divorce as a solution, Kimberly said Stephen would be so emotionally distraught he'd probably kill himself, negating any chance for her to inherit his $450,000 life insurance policy. At the time her friends thought the talk about killing her husband was a joke, and that she was simply blowing off steam. But following Stephen's death, investigators learned that Kimberly's plan had deep roots, so deep that one friend testified that Kimberly claimed she could get a drug that would paralyze her husband and stop his breathing, during which time she'd set fire to the room, ostensibly to show that Stephen died from smoke inhalation.

Additionally, a coworker at Holy Cross Hospital told investigators how Kimberly surprised him one day with a request: She wanted him to kill her husband. He, too, like the others, thought it was a joke, until Kimberly offered him $50,000. The friend declined. Kimberly told him to "forget about it" and to keep their conversation a secret. At that point Kimberly decided to take matters into her own hands.

Prosecutors said that upon Kimberly and Stephen's return to their cottage following the dinner theater Kimberly injected her husband with succinylcholine, a drug found only in operating rooms, which causes instant paralysis and, in larger doses, death. Succinylcholine also wears off after just a few minutes and is virtually untraceable.

Kimberly, intending to paralyze her husband and see to his death via smoke inhalation, instead injected him with a far greater dosage, which killed him almost immediately. She then placed his six-foot-three, 245-pound body on the floor between the twin beds, resting his head on two pillows, which she set on fire. She left behind a cigar to give the impression that Stephen had been smoking in bed. Kimberly left the room, and then returned, ignoring neighboring cottages to run across the road to the front desk, where she coolly told employees there that her cottage was on fire. There was no emotion in her voice then or after they pulled her badly burned and dead husband out of the room. Kimberly's only concern over the next week was ensuring that Stephen was cremated.

With no blood alcohol level, investigators knew Stephen had not drunk that night. And he didn't smoke. Investigators tracked the package of cigars to the store where it was purchased, and discovered that Kimberly had bought it.

Three months after Stephen's death, Kimberly was charged with his murder. She was later tried, found guilty, and sentenced to life in prison.

KILLING for money, power, and material gain has been happening since the beginning of time, and women are certainly among such killers. To deny that women kill for money is not true. The reality is that people do not always make the wisest decisions when it comes to greed and taking care of themselves. The Black Widow and the Profit Killer have been studied in depth by researchers. What shocks the public about these killers is that they seem to defy our image of women as being naturally wired to be "all good" mothers and nurturing life partners. These women are also thought to be some of the most intelligent, imaginative, and vigilant killers when it comes to domestic homicide. In fact, many such crimes go undetected because they are so cleverly executed. These lady killers are known to use a variety of methods to murder and tend to be dispassionate about the homicides they commit.

According to the book *Female Crime and Delinquency,* by Coramae Richey Mann, women have always been viewed as psychologically different from men. In a classic study conducted by Cesare Lombroso and William Ferrero, females were observed as encompassing "all the criminal qualities of the male plus all the worst characteristics of women, namely cunning, spite, and deceitfulness." Some of these earlier authors even believed that women may be more cruel, vengeful, cold, and ferocious than men.

Professor Otto Pollack refers to a few reasons he thinks that women can get away with crimes more easily than their male counterparts. He believes this is due to underreporting, underdetection, and the paternalism of the police and the court system. Pollack's views take on a more suspicious tone when he suggests that female criminality is masked and that women, especially criminal women, are deceitful by nature. He believes that their deceitful and manipulative ways are encouraged by their ability to fake orgasms, feign sexual pleasure, and pretend to desire a man. Concealment of their monthly menses, in his estimation, also indicates women's inherent ability to be secretive, which makes them difficult to trust. Since the 1970s there has been an increasing and disturbing rise of violent crimes committed by women, and this rise may suggest something has drastically changed in our society.

Historically women have always been viewed as either good or bad, and such views seemed to lack any middle ground. Sometimes this dichotomy has been understood in terms of the Madonna/whore duality, or attitudes that stem from Judeo-Christian ideology or pagan mythology. It may also be based on the way men are affected by a woman's sexuality. The Madonna aspect of a woman refers to her ability to produce children and maintain the family unit. The whore side of the duality suggests that a woman's power to excite a man's passions, thus interfering with his ability to control himself, makes her very dangerous.

In modern society women are frequently viewed as victims when a homicide occurs within the context of an intimate or marital relationship. American culture also has a tendency to view a woman as weak compared to the domineering, all-powerful, and overcontrolling man. Women have even enjoyed more lenient sentencing because of the idea that they are less malevolent than men and hence are more prone to be dominated by them. Women are still considered more likely to feel remorse for their crimes than are their male equivalents. Although this may be so in some cases, in others, such as that of Kimberly Hricko, it could not be further from the truth.

Kimberly was as dispassionate as they come. While not a stereotypical Black Widow, her lack of remorse after carefully carrying out the murder of her husband clearly makes her a Profit Killer. After all, she felt bored by him. Shouldn't a passionless marriage be grounds for murder anyway? Kimberly had tried to talk with friends about her restlessness and her miserable marriage, but they never really had any good recommendations for her. They would tell her to divorce her husband. Divorce? Then how would she get all the money from his insurance plan?

Kimberly felt entitled to get what she wanted. The problem is, she did not have the idea that she should have to pay the consequences of the "wrong" choices she had made. If she got divorced, she would not get the same amount of money as she would if her husband were dead. She was not prepared to take responsibility for her choices, hence she felt entitled to get everything she wanted, even if it meant she had to commit murder. She needed to erase who she did not want in her life so she could survive and thrive.

Kimberly experienced her husband as stopping her from having the life she wanted and was meant to have. He was simply in the way. Her affair confirmed how she was supposed to feel in a relationship. Her new lover made her feel sexy. This only supported her conviction that her husband had only one place in her life, in the ground six feet under and away from her. Only when her husband was dead could she enjoy the big fat insurance check that was meant to be hers. If she plotted things correctly, she could have her freedom and a nice amount of money to boot.

She just knew it, but first her husband had to die.

6

The Narcissistic Killer

ACCORDING to Greek myth, Narcissus was a boy who fell madly in love with his reflection in the surface of a pond. Because of his intense self-love he rejected the advances of the nymph Echo. As punishment for callously rejecting Echo he was cursed by the gods to endlessly pine for himself even as he fell deeper in love with his own unobtainable image. Narcissus longed for this unattainable spirit until he could stand it no more. He ultimately jumped into the water and drowned. The ill-fated Narcissus came to symbolize the unfortunate plight of those addicted to a malevolent self-love. This condition is believed to cause a narcissistic personality disorder, and in many cases irreversible self-destruction.

The person who suffers from a narcissistic personality disorder does not really love himself but only seems to. What he really loves is the reflection of himself or the image he projects. Loving the reflection, as opposed to the true or core self, poses several problems. When someone has this type of personality disorder, he overly depends on the availability of his reflection in order to feel self-love and self-acceptance. Because there is no realistic yardstick to judge his image it is impossible to tell whether it is accurate or not.

Instead of loving themselves, in reality narcissists only love other people's impressions of them. They crave admiration and are junkies for positive feedback from others. It is through the reaction of others that the narcissist experiences himself. When narcissists do not get the desired reaction, it becomes virtually impossible for them to feel whole or complete, equivalent to feeling that without a mirror to reflect oneself, there is no self. The healthy individual knows that he exists, whether a mirror is there to reflect his image or not.

Although there is a genetic component to this type of personality disorder, environment also plays a significant role. The person with this disorder feels disappointed, hurt, and failed by his/her original caretakers. Instead of relying on others to love him/her, afflicted individuals decide loving themselves is the best way to feel love without being neglected or hurt. Many narcissists decide early on that the only reliable person is himself. Relationships are painful for the narcissist, which, as previously discussed, makes intimacy virtually unachievable.

Every personality has a narcissistic element. It is the part of our psyche that loves ourselves unconditionally. If it stays in check, this kind of self-love can actually be quite healthy and help us to survive. But if narcissism becomes pathological, it can be potentially lethal for both the narcissist and those around him.

Individuals who suffer from a narcissistic personality disorder tend to regard and treat other people as objects to be exploited. People are just there to feed their ego and provide them with a narcissistic supply otherwise known as constant adulation. Narcissists believe themselves entitled to "special" treatment because of their grandiose fantasies about themselves. This type of personality is not self-aware, and emotions and thoughts are greatly distorted as a result.

The narcissist is usually the first victim of his own mental disability, which often prevents him from enjoying life and having mature and adult relationships. Many narcissists are emotionally paralyzed. Such a person is a master of disguise and therefore difficult to identify. Narcissists tend to be charming but haughty. They often fantasize about unlimited success and brag incessantly while ignoring others and not listening. They also have a habit of humiliating, criticizing, and belittling others, whose only function is to admire and assure them that they exist. They're junkies for compliments and they attack people who they believe take them for granted, or who fail to recognize their greatness and superiority. For the narcissist, this group includes just about everyone.

Those they attract as lovers need the narcissist's dramatic take on life and tend to fade into the background, learning the art of un-being. Such partners are often addicted and attracted to the excitement and violation of routine, and live vicariously through their narcissistic partner. One downside of this type of partnership is that the wishes of the narcissist's partner matter little. The partner has one function only—to become a feeder or pusher of the narcissist's unending need to feel extraordinary.

When the narcissist feels burdened, cornered, suffocated, or trapped, he is compelled to abandon his commitment. And when the intimate partner in the narcissist's life is no longer of value, he/she is then in danger of being discarded. For the murderous narcissist, this can be a pivotal and dangerous time.

• • •

Such was the case of Rabbi FRED NEULANDER, the fiery yet compassionate leader of the Congregation M'Kor Shalom in affluent Cherry Hill, New Jersey.

Rabbi Neulander was trusted and revered; he fulfilled the spiritual needs of the thousand or so families in the congregation he founded. Neulander was an inspiration, a man who for thirty years had been married to his college sweetheart, Carol, who he met at Trinity College in New Jersey in the 1960s. Carol supported her husband during the early years when he founded Congregation M'Kor Shalom, and they had raised three children together. She later became a successful businesswoman, managing two bakeries. But her family's focus was always her husband, who was an icon in their community, a man who presided over weddings and funerals and other life events, and who served as the spiritual backbone for so many.

So it came as a great shock and surprise when Carol was murdered in November 1994, and of even greater surprise when her husband was arrested in 1998 and charged with hiring two hit men to murder his wife.

The crime was particularly gruesome. When Neulander returned home that night from his office he found Carol lying on the living room floor, bludgeoned and bloodied, the victim of an apparent attack, perhaps by burglars. At first no one suspected that he was behind his wife's tragic death, even after police learned that the well-respected rabbi was involved in an affair with a popular Philadelphia radio deejay. But as investigators dug deeper into Neulander's life they discovered a man not only revered by the community, but one who revered himself. A man of such arrogance, prosecutors later concluded, was no more than a manipulative adulterer who had decided to kill his wife to continue another relationship.

It was, they said, all about *him*.

To prove their point, prosecutors interviewed the "other woman," Elaine Soncini, a Philadelphia woman who met Rabbi

Neulander as her husband was dying in 1992. Neulander was there to comfort her, but soon they began a torrid affair, often meeting in her apartment and even in his office at the synagogue.

For two years Neulander serenaded Soncini with passionate phone calls and love poems, professing his undying devotion to her while also expressing some disturbing thoughts and ideas concerning his wife. Soncini later testified during Neulander's first trial that he said he dreamed of his wife dying. Following Carol's murder, Neulander told Soncini, "I told you to trust me. When God closes a door, he opens a window." But in reality it was Neulander, believing *he* was God, who closed the door on Carol's life.

During his second trial in 2003 (his first trial, in 2000, had ended in a hung jury) two men testified that Neulander had hired them to kill his wife. Len Jenoff, fifty-six, and Paul Michael Daniels, twenty-six, said Neulander initially promised Jenoff $30,000 to kill "an enemy of Israel." Jenoff would soon learn the real target was Carol Neulander. Jenoff, who told Neulander that he was an ex–CIA agent, agreed to the plan and brought in his roommate Daniels, a drug addict, alcoholic, and paranoid schizophrenic. Neulander gave Jenoff a $7,500 down payment, and they concocted a plan whereby Neulander would be working at the temple while Jenoff and Daniels would visit the Neulander home pretending to be deliverymen.

On the night of the murder, with Carol home alone, the two men knocked on the front door. When she let them in, Jenoff later testified, he put his hand on her shoulder so she couldn't turn around and hit her in the head with a lead pipe. Dazed, Carol asked, "Why, why?" before Daniels hit her two more times. When her husband found her dead, lying in a pool of blood, he didn't take her pulse or even touch her, telling investigators that he was "too shocked" to do much of anything.

Rabbi Neulander's son Matthew testified that when he arrived on the scene his father was "blank and unemotional." There was no heavy breathing or crying. Neulander's children would also testify that their mother was angry and bitter toward their father, and wanted him out of the house. Fearing a divorce would lessen his standing with his congregation, Neulander decided on a different tack, prosecutors said.

Neulander, believing his ability to inspire a large group of people would work in front of a jury, hurt his case when he decided to testify. He was unemotional, uncaring, and arrogant, and that lack of emotion shown toward a wife of thirty years was enough to convince a jury he was, in fact, involved in her death. In addition, a former racquetball partner testified that Neulander told him several months before the murder that he wished he could "get rid of his wife."

Despite the guilty verdict, Neulander has steadfastly maintained his innocence. During the penalty phase of his trial he spoke to the jury for nearly twenty-five minutes, hoping to convince them that he deserved to live. He was preaching again, only this time instead of repairing and uplifting the spiritual health of a congregation, Neulander fought for his own life, expressing his love for his dead wife, even going so far as to say he missed her. But the "sermon" infuriated his family, and two of his children, Matthew and Rebecca, said afterward he was evil and a fiend. A brother-in-law even asked the judge to sentence him to anonymity so that he could "suffer his narcissism in silence."

Neulander escaped death, and was instead sentenced to life in prison.

But following the sentencing, in an interview on ABC with Barbara Walters that served only to anger all connected to the case, Neulander again claimed his innocence and expressed his own deep "intense rage."

He was, he said, the real victim in this case.

• • •

NARCISSISTS believe they are the center of the world, not just their own personal world, but the entire world, and Rabbi Fred Neulander was clearly at the center of his world. In addition to believing they were born with a silver spoon in their mouth, narcissists also believe that the coveted Oscar should be given to them inevitably at birth, just because they have been born.

Neulander felt he was above the law, that rules applied to other people who were not as gifted and fantastic as he was. He also felt entitled to doing and getting whatever he wanted in life. This included killing his wife Carol.

Although useful at one point to his life and career, Carol had lost her value. She was the good wife as he worked his way toward becoming a successful rabbi, and a good-enough wife to give him three beautiful children. But now it was a different story. He was a *star* and Carol was no longer good enough. He needed to be with a star like himself, like his radio deejay lover, Elaine Soncini. She knew his worth. She was on his level. She was even willing to convert to Judaism for him. There was a gap between what his life was and what it should be. The only explanation, according to Fred Neulander's psyche, was that it was his wife's fault.

Interestingly, narcissists do not deal well with intimacy. Their problem stems from a sense of individual uniqueness. Being unique and being intimate are strong adversaries. Intimacy is a common pursuit for almost everyone; therefore its seeker is not unique. Intimacy also makes it hard for a person to feel superior because it demystifies him. Demystification is something the narcissist tries to avoid at all costs. It's also hard to be intimate when you are lying. This narcissist personality tends to deceive others on practically every aspect of his life, including emotions, history, self, avocations, and vocations.

Fred Neulander was able to live with his wife as long as she catered to his needs and doted on his exceptional personality. She also had to play the supportive and ideal wife in order for him to remain fulfilled. But once reality entered into his relationship, he found it ordinary and boring, given how self-important he was. Neulander needed more excitement and could no longer remain with such an average person, or in such an average relationship. He became angry and he was convinced his anger was justified. He directed that anger squarely at his wife, who deserved to be punished for failing him. She was no longer the adoring, obedient, and docile wife he once knew. He could no longer settle for a person who failed to recognize his cosmic significance and uniqueness in the world. In fact, according to his worldview, ordinary people hold back greatness, and Carol was probably holding him back from the fame and wealth he was truly entitled to and, more important, destined for.

Generally speaking, the only feelings that matter to the narcissist are his own. When Carol threatened her husband with divorce and exposure to the community and with him fearing that she would take him to the cleaners financially, Neulander believed he had reason enough to eliminate her. That, of course, put him at odds with his position as a rabbi—a leader who supposedly provided comfort and hope. Yet there was nothing religious about Fred Neulander. Serving as a rabbi was a job, not a religious calling or commitment. He was controlling and power hungry and had no real sense of anyone else. He used the pulpit like he used other people, simply to get what he wanted.

The narcissist, you see, rarely converses but often lectures. He never just walks, he poses. In its more benign form the narcissist is condescending, posturing, or teaching. In its more severe form the narcissist is humiliating, sadistic, impatient, and full of rage and righteousness. When angry the narcissist displays cynicism, disgust, and repulsion.

With the grandiose state of mind the narcissist believes he/she knows what people want and need from him/her. Narcissists also tend to have a messianic complex in that they believe they know what is right for society and never question what they're doing, whether it is good or right. And therein lies part of the problem. (A messianic complex used to be viewed as a psychological sickness that reflected an individual's delusional belief that he or she was the Messiah.)

Neulander in particular acted as sole judge and jury, much like God. His thinking process led him to believe that by working with God, he himself became God-like. Only he was a vengeful God. If you look at the Old Testament, compared to the New Testament, God is often portrayed as a testing and vengeful force as opposed to a loving and accepting one. Neulander was even too good to kill his wife himself; he used his powers to manipulate an adoring fan to do his dirty work for him.

Neulander also felt a need to conquer many women, serially, in order to maintain his feeling of being powerful. He never really felt committed to anyone unless she gave him the admiration and attention he felt entitled to and needed so desperately. Many of the women who he had affairs with he converted to Judaism, which again underscored his God-like complex, *"I will show you the way and change you."*

Neulander was one of the bad guys in life, masquerading as a healer. One irony is, as one of the most popular rabbis in his local area, it was very possible he managed to be helpful to some people. He could offer his congregation hope, a very powerful and therapeutic emotion. Neulander communicated to the people the faith he had in himself. This belief and its effect on his congregation was so powerful that people wanted more of it because they believed it would wear off on them. Neulander's strength was his ability to manipulate people.

It is said that narcissists don't feel they exist unless they have an audience that is reacting to them. This audience, in turn, needs and feeds off the glowing reflection it reflects back to the narcissist. Without this the narcissist feels empty and nonexistent.

Even during his final performance, his trial, Neulander thought he could sway all with his brilliance. When he took the stand to testify in his defense he was mesmerizing, charismatic, charming, and clever. He also justified everything, so convincingly that you wanted to believe him. His words had a magical and hypnotic quality. He made you feel that humanity, especially in the guise of a highly respected religious leader, could never be so dark and evil.

But he was.

Pamela Smart was also very calculating. But Pamela, much like the rabbi, could not escape the awful truth.

On the evening of May 1, 1990, Derry, New Hampshire, police entered the condominium she shared with her husband Gregory. He was lying facedown on the floor, his body twisted, a bullet hole behind his ear. Pamela, twenty-two, had found his body after returning home from a school board meeting. She ran through the neighborhood screaming, knocking on doors, and begging for help. When police arrived they surveyed the crime scene, but the detectives thought something was odd. There were no signs of a struggle and, more important, in a small town like Derry, burglars rarely packed a gun. The home had apparently been burglarized, with clothes strewn throughout and jewelry missing, yet it became apparent to officials that the "burglary" had been staged. Since Greg, twenty-three, had been shot once behind the ear, execution style, the real motive, police believed, was murder. A list of suspects was assembled, and Pamela's name soon rose to the top of that list.

Nothing immediately jumped out at police to cause them to

focus on the young wife. Instead, it was the little things, such as Pamela's concern for the couple's dog while her husband's body lay cold and still on the living room carpet. And when she returned home the next day with a police escort to retrieve some personal items, Pamela callously stepped on the bloodstained carpeting—the very spot where her husband had fallen. It was clear to police that Pamela Smart was no grieving widow.

As the investigation proceeded police would learn that, indeed, there was more to Pamela Smart than they could have imagined. As it turned out, Pamela choreographed her husband's murder by seducing a 16-year-old student, Billy Flynn, and encouraging him to kill Greg.

PAMELA and Greg had wed only a year earlier. He was an insurance salesman, following in his father's footsteps. Pamela was a high school cheerleader and honor student who graduated from college a year early with designs on becoming a television reporter.

The second of three children, Pamela was close to her mother but distant from her father, who was a pilot. She loved being the center of attention. She was also compulsively organized, from her clothing to her schedule, and she got angry when her life was disorganized in any way. She met Greg at a New Year's Eve party and they quickly hit it off, sharing a love of heavy metal music. With his shoulder-length hair, Greg appeared rebellious, which attracted Pamela even more. They married in 1989, but trouble soon followed. Through his job as an insurance salesman Greg drifted toward new friends, eventually confessing to an affair. Pamela was devastated. She grew distant from her husband, and she told friends she couldn't trust him. She decided to focus her attention on her career and her job as the media services director with the Hampton, New Hampshire, school board. It was there where she met Billy Flynn, a student at Winnacunnet High School, during an exercise on teenage self-esteem. Flynn became infatuated with the "older" woman and she sensed his attraction. Pamela courted Flynn, giving him an envelope containing photos of her posing in her underwear. They soon became intimate, and the sex drew Flynn further into Pamela's web. She even talked with Flynn of a life together. But she had a problem: her husband.

Pamela prodded Flynn to "get rid of" Greg, but Flynn suggested that she should divorce her husband. Pamela said no, that she would lose her home and Greg would stalk her, making her life a living hell. She finally laid it on the line, telling Flynn that if he wanted to continue their relationship, he would have to kill Greg. Two plans to murder Greg were set, but failed when the teenager got cold feet. Pamela was infuriated, but she gave Flynn one more chance to prove his love.

On the night of May 1, Flynn and a friend were given a key by Pamela and waited inside the Smart home for Greg to return from work. Pamela, coincidentally, was at a school board meeting. The teens first tossed the Smarts' dog, Halen, into the basement, and then trashed the house, hoping to give the appearance that a burglary had been committed. As soon as Greg opened the door and stepped inside, the two boys grabbed him and threw him to the floor. Flynn put the gun to Greg's head, said, "God forgive me," and fired once.

After police zeroed in on Pamela, they wired up one of her high school interns, who caught Pamela on tape discussing the murder and the aftermath. Pamela was arrogant, manipulative, and cold, telling the intern that police would never suspect her, a woman with a "professional reputation."

"They're going to believe me," she said.

She was subsequently arrested, tried, found guilty, and is serving a life term with no chance for parole at the Bedford Correctional Facility in New York.

Clara Harris

David Brame

Dr. Robert Bierenbaum and his wife Janet leave court.

Dr. Richard Sharpe shown in this undated family photo with his daughter Alexandra, 4, and son Michael, 8.

Christian Longo

Mark Hacking
(left) with his
wife, Lori

Lynn Turner

Kimberly Hricko

Rabbi Fred Neulander

Pamela Smart and her husband Gregory on their wedding day.

Laci and Scott Peterson are shown in a photo taken during the 2002 Christmas season in Modesto, California.

Michael Peterson, left, alongside his son, Todd Peterson, and adopted daughter, Margaret Ratliff, listen to a hearing after trial on Friday, August 8, 2003.

Susan Wright

Nancy Seaman

Rae Carruth

Charles Stewart

• • •

PAMELA Smart had all of the characteristics of a classic narcissist. By her own admission she was incredibly egocentric. She loved being the center of attention and prided herself on her ability to capture the limelight. She would say, "I'm definitely a typical Leo." Leo is an astrological sign noted for its charismatic and regal characteristics, and its symbol, the lion, represents the king or queen of the jungle.

Like many young couples who fall hard and fast and then get married, disappointment soon followed. Greg was supposed to be an exciting rocker boy and Pamela thought she was going to be the Jerry Hall to his Mick Jagger. She also had visions of being the beautiful, successful television reporter who had the cool bad-boy husband, but what she got instead was very different. Marriage changed Greg, and Pamela didn't like the change. Instead of maintaining the characteristics that attracted her, he went in a completely opposite direction.

Love means something different to everyone. To Pamela Smart, it meant her partner would be like herself. When he changed, that was the first major crack in their already fragile relationship. He became conservative and joined his father's insurance business. Although he was ambitious, a salesman was not what Pamela wanted. In fact, that was the antithesis of the rocker husband she envisioned for herself. Where was the man she fell in love with? She felt like she was married to a stranger—a stranger she did not particularly like. The man she loved had left her. She felt betrayed.

Once Greg changed his lifestyle, he wanted his wife to change, too. He wanted to settle down and raise a family. Even worse, as the couple reached their first anniversary Greg admitted to having an affair. It is hard to know what motivated his infidelity. Did he have an affair because Pamela was critical of him? Was he sensing their marriage was on the rocks? Did he have an affair because he wanted to feel the love and approval he no longer felt from his wife? Was he trying to send a message to Pamela that he needed her to be different, more loving and domestic, less self-centered and professionally driven? We will never know for sure, but admitting the affair was the beginning of the end of the Smart marriage.

It is not uncommon for people to change once they marry. Many revert back to an image in their mind, to an original model of a father or a mother, or married couple. There is something almost compulsive about such changes. These marital rituals trigger something in the brain that makes us go on autopilot. Pamela, who had her own set of personality deficits, expected her husband to meet her needs. In a healthy marriage both partners give to each other so both can feel restored. This was not happening in the Smart marriage, so Pamela was going to take matters into her own hands. She would meet her own needs and her plan did not include Greg. In fact, Greg had betrayed her emotionally and sexually in every way possible. He did not offer her the status she wanted and needed. Greg Smart had messed with the wrong woman, and he was going to pay. He should have known better. Now he really deserved to die.

Passion has always been somewhat risky and dangerous. Once the idealizations of marriage give way to the realities of life together, it can feel mundane and unfulfilling, especially for the narcissist who wants way more than that out of life. Such an individual firmly believes in her own uniqueness and specialness, and as a result, requires excessive admiration and attention. Greg was not giving Pamela this attention, so she had to find it for herself elsewhere. That is where Billy Flynn came into the picture.

Although Pamela Smart was not a teacher, she exhibited some of the same psychological characteristics of adult teachers who have affairs with their students. Billy Flynn, like many students who have affairs with their teachers, exuded psychological vulnerabilities. He was inclined to see Pamela as the nurturing figure he did not have. Students who have affairs with their teachers often have low self-esteem and a pattern of difficulties with personal relationships. Teachers who engage in these types of illicit romantic affairs have their own set of psychological vulnerabilities. Pamela showed the familiar teacher/student psychological profile. It was a time in her life when she was beginning to question her own attractiveness or value after her husband's affair. She needed to test herself. Conditions at home increased her need to be needed. When a teacher or mentor experiences difficulties in her home life, it can become very tempting to reach out to a student, who at the very least respects what she does and who she is as a person. Students are inclined to idealize the teacher. For Pamela Smart this was perfect. She liked being idealized. And like most good narcissists, she went over the top. Instead of simply securing just one loyal student to boost her failing self-image, she decided to create a club of groupies, the more members the better.

This group included other disturbed youths who would also become vulnerable to her power and position. Teacher/mentors can become god- and goddesslike figures. Pamela Smart manipulated these students and used her professional position to achieve her own personal and ultimately murderous desires. She became drunk on her power and lost all sense of reality. She thought she could get away with murder.

In many ways Pamela had stopped growing. She was emotionally arrested and regressed at this adolescent stage, so mentally or psychologically, she was not that much different from the teenagers she befriended. These students could afford to be long-haired bad boys. They were too young to have to deal with the realities and pressures of married life, as did her husband, Greg. They were her loyal fans, and as such, had not disappointed her—at least not yet. This rebellious, adolescent time of life had become a part of Pamela's identity more than her real age of twenty-two. Being around these students heightened her sense of belonging in that glorious and carefree moment, the time when she felt most alive, powerful, and special. Everything going on during this stage of life felt new; it was a feeling that was almost impossible to beat.

Like many adults who engage in student/teacher romances, Pamela suffered from psychological issues such as impulse control disorder, mood disorder, hypersexuality, an underdeveloped personality, and feelings of inadequacy and depression.

From Pamela's perspective Billy Flynn and the other students knew what she was worth. This further supported her grandiose notion that her plan to kill her husband was justified. Plus, it felt good to have people be willing to do anything for her. This is what celebrities have. People will do anything for them. And Pamela deserved nothing less, for she, too, was a celebrity reporter on the brink of discovery, only no one had discovered her yet. What Pamela did not realize was that she was producing and starring in her own murder trial. Not exactly what she had in mind, but it was the role of a lifetime that would land her in prison.

Ultimately, Pamela Smart suffered from a form of narcissism in which, underneath it all, she was consumed with guilt. Such narcissists falsely believe they can do whatever they want and get away with it. They take unusual risks and then expect the miraculous to happen. That is one of the reasons they are so shocked when their fantasies remain just that—fantasies. They temporarily distract themselves from reality when they construct a pleasing audience, but this usually does not last for very long. It is also not an adequate solution to their underlying problems. They tend to internalize and give a lot of power to the meaningful voices from their past who scolded them and told them they were worthless. These are the voices and opinions they really believe. Therefore, on some deep level, they feel deserving of punishment and retaliation.

This is why their lives often look like an ongoing trial, even if in reality there is no trial. When her spousal homicide plan backfired, and Pamela was made to answer for her immoral behavior, she could tell herself she was just the object of abuse and envy. That is really why people wanted to destroy her. It would not be surprising if Pamela Smart chooses to deny her role in her fate and her life until the day she dies. There is a good chance that she will convince herself of her alibi and that she is really one of life's sad and unfortunate victims. Cursed to endure a horrible fate, just like Narcissus.

7

The Temper Tantrum Killer

TEMPER tantrums are normally reserved to unruly infants during the terrible twos. It is not particularly uncommon, however, for immature adults to have temper tantrums.

People who never develop beyond "the world is all about me" phase can be especially susceptible to acting out this way. Combining such a personality defect with a series of frustrating or undesirable situations can translate to murder.

Some adults who suffer from a lack of control are diagnosed with intermittent explosive disorder, a psychological problem defined by extreme problems with impulse control. Individuals with IED are prone to aggressive outbursts under extreme duress. They perceive the stress as a threat, an insult, frustration, a vulnerability, or a combination of all these. There may be some unusual brain wave patterns as well as some "soft" neurological findings in these people, but the disorder is primarily triggered when perceived needs are not met.

The Temper Tantrum Killer has acquired experiences early in life when his bad behaviors were tolerated, and these behaviors continue into adulthood. However, a small percentage of individuals develop this pattern of behavior suddenly without any prior history. The person suffering from intermittent explosive disorder is usually upset, remorseful, and feels very guilty instantly after a rageful episode. During the moment, however, he/she feels rehabilitated by this aggressive release.

The individual afflicted with intermittent explosive disorder tends to be male. He blames others for his behavior as a way to avoid changing and/or to justify or alleviate his guilt.

A man who loses control only in his significant relationship tends to give emotional ultimatums to his partner. He may expect his spouse to behave, think, or respond in a very specific way. If his expectation is not met, the tension in the relationship can increase. Ultimately this individual's ability to maintain control is lost. Since expectations placed on an intimate relationship are not placed on other relationships, the immature, irrational, and sometimes violent behavior is expressed exclusively within the marital relationship.

Unlike the narcissistic killer, who harms those who no longer fill his needs, the Temper Tantrum Killer, having never developed a mature manner of reasoning during difficult or stressful situations, explodes in a fit of rage when things don't go his way.

When you mix this kind of personality defect with a series of frustrating or undesirable situations, the combination can be deadly.

SUCH was the case of SCOTT PETERSON.

His was a story unlike any other, a tragic tale that captured the attention of the American public like no case since the O. J.

Simpson murder trial. Scott and Laci Peterson were a beautiful couple, often described by family and friends as the object of envy. But like many marriages that end in murder, underneath the picture-perfect façade was a dark and ugly truth that no one saw or even imagined.

We are very often fooled by attractive couples. If they appear beautiful and happy, we are inclined to believe our eyes. Scott and Laci looked like that cute couple in college who could be friends with anyone. They could have been our next-door neighbors. It was not hard to see why Laci found Scott appealing. He was good-looking, confident, sexy, and very romantic. He had a magical way about him, and Laci fell head over heels in love. Every conversation they had seemed intimate and intense. Laci felt elevated and adored; the connection between the two of them was impossible to miss. It's ironic that their first date took place on a boat and that she became seasick, an ominous portent of her fate.

After meeting in college and marrying, the couple settled in northern California, where Scott worked as a fertilizer salesman and Laci as a substitute teacher. Laci was happy and bubbly, with an infectious spirit. The couple was expecting their first child when, on Christmas Eve 2003, Laci disappeared.

Scott said he had last seen his wife that morning when he left their Modesto home for the ninety-minute drive to San Francisco Bay, where he went fishing. Laci, he said, was planning to go grocery shopping. But when he returned home, she was gone, though personal items such as her cell phone and purse were in the house. A massive search ensued, involving police and hundreds of volunteers. Laci's family even posted a $500,000 reward for information about her whereabouts.

Scott played the role of the distraught husband, taking part in the search for his missing wife, but within weeks the shocking truth about Scott came to light as police learned that he was involved with another woman, Amber Frey. It was Amber, a massage therapist previously unaware that Scott was married, who recognized him from the daily TV reports and who called police.

In mid-April the body of Laci and her unborn son Conner washed up on the shoreline near where Scott claimed he'd gone fishing the day Laci disappeared. He was arrested a week later, near his parents' home in San Diego, and charged with two counts of murder. In 2005, as the world watched, he was convicted of murdering his wife and unborn son and sentenced to death.

IT has been said many times that part of the reason many of us found this case so compelling was the appearance of the Petersons, who looked like a couple that had everything going for them. In essence, they seemed like the all-American couple "next door," and that they weren't at all served to underscore that things are rarely what they seem.

The Peterson case also raised a very important question: How well do we really know our brother, our friend, our family members? What really goes on in the lives of people we *think* we know? This case was a brutal reminder that much in life is often nothing more than an illusion. For example, Scott suffered from low self-control and egocentricity, and yet part of what made him so exciting to Laci and the people who loved him was his hedonistic approach to life.

One of the down sides to this pleasure-seeking approach to life is that it made Scott completely self-absorbed. He vehemently demanded that his own satisfactions be met above everyone else's. Scott's self-regulation skills were greatly impaired. He had the classic narcissistic and sociopathic personality features, which made him dangerous under the "best" conditions. What his wife, friends, and family did not know, at least at first, was that his ability to tolerate frustration was no better than a toddler's. When a toddler cannot have a toy he wants, he will fly into a rage and then imagine annihilating the outside source of that rage.

Scott exhibited several characteristics which, in retrospect, seem all the more alarming. His approach to life was shortsighted, and he had poor judgment and planning skills. He sought immediate and easy pleasure and avoided pain whenever he could. When his behavior was not tolerated he thought nothing of lying, hiding, suppressing, or disguising his self-serving approach to life. His charismatic social presence helped to camouflage his moral impairments. His charm was the equivalent of a local anesthetic, to help ease the pain he invariably caused. Such characteristics are a recipe for disaster if they aren't dealt with at an early age. In Scott Peterson's case, the combination turned deadly.

Men who kill their wives typically have not killed anyone before and probably will not kill anyone else. If you look closely, you would find a certain derogatory set of feelings and attitudes toward women in general. For example, women are often viewed as property that has no rights. This attitude can be manifested in many different ways, including cheating (which is a form of psychological abandonment and abuse), verbal abuse, and physical expressions of anger and aggression.

Very often such men wish that their wives would die, or at the very least they like the idea of having a dead wife. Scott told Amber Frey a few weeks before his wife went missing that he was a widower and that the upcoming Christmas would be his first without her. If you look at the fantasy life of these intimate-partner killers, you may even find that they think about violently evening the score against anyone who crosses them.

Scott Peterson's story did not ring true from the very beginning. If he did not want his wife dead, who did? Laci was a young woman eight months pregnant and readying herself for a magical moment in her life. Her husband was clearly the most likely candidate. His television interviews revealed an oddly "fake" emotional quality. His tears seemed false, badly acted, typical of people with antisocial personality disorders. They don't feel things like the rest of us, so when they pretend to have a strong emotion, it appears false.

After Laci's disappearance, Scott's behavior was also unusual in other ways. He said he went fishing alone, on Christmas Eve no less. He then tried to sell their house and car right away and even ordered porn movies, something Laci would never have allowed. Laci's family also had their growing suspicions, especially after learning their son-in-law had an affair prior to his pregnant wife's disappearance.

The motive for removing Laci from his life was now coming into full view. Scott didn't want to be a father or a husband. He wanted to be free.

SCOTT was the only son of Lee and Jackie Peterson. He had several half siblings, but Scott was the youngest. He would be described by his half sister, Ann Bird, who had been given away by Jackie Peterson at birth, as the "special child" or "golden boy." He could do no wrong and the family treated him like a little prince. Such treatment gave young Scott the idea that he was, in fact, special and *should* receive special attention and abide by a different set of rules than everyone else. Naturally, over time, Scott's sense of entitlement warped his view of the world. If his own parents did not say no to him, he figured, why let anyone else say no to him?

This type of character defect makes it very hard to tolerate frustration. Criminals tend to have two extreme family dynamics; either they were terribly abused as children and therefore feel entitled to whatever they can take in later life, or they were overly indulged, giving them the idea that they deserve whatever they desire. Scott learned early on that he was entitled not for *doing,* but for *being.* It was his Peterson birthright. He was an aristocrat in his own mind.

According to theorist Karen Horney, the spoiled or smothered child is really dehumanized and instrumentalized. The parents love the child not really for what he/she is, but who they want or imagine him/her to be. The child is there to fulfill their dreams, and becomes a way to magically transform the parents' dissatisfied lives into successes. As a result spoiled children often give up reality to adopt their parental fantasies. In the womb of these fantasies they feel worthy, perfect, and entitled. Such children are unable to realistically assess their true abilities and limitations. Neither can they understand the expectations of others, the value of teamwork, and perhaps most important they do not have the ability to postpone gratification. The family is the first and most important teacher of our identity and source of emotional support. It is the place we learn to feel cared for and loved, and it forms the template for all future relationships. Therefore, as the spoiled or smothered child grows up, he almost always feels rage when people repeatedly fail to live up to his very high and unrealistic expectations.

In many ways human development is very much like that of a tree. If a tree cannot grow in one direction, it bends and shifts its branches around whatever obstacle is in the way until it finds balance and equilibrium. Psychopathology is a result of a disturbed growth. It is an adaptive attempt to grow around obstacles. Psychological growth crises stunt human development. With this in mind, Scott Peterson was no different from a two-year-old screaming to get his way. Of course a screaming two-year-old is far less lethal than a tantruming adult.

This also explains Scott's disenchantment with his impending fatherhood. He was still emotionally a child himself and felt unable to tolerate the responsibilities inherent in childrearing. Laci's pregnancy had been more *her* idea than his anyway. She was always far more ready to jump into the next phase of their lives than he was. Her pregnancy made him feel trapped, edgy, and ultimately violent. He also felt Laci was acting different. In the past she had been far more lenient about his "flaws and imperfections." He could get away with having affairs more easily. It was much easier for him to please her by doing nothing much in particular. But now she was turning into Martha Stewart number 2. She was on his case all the time. Their marriage was like *House Beautiful* meets *Animal House*. Her demands were getting more intense and he hated it. If this was the way life was going to be, it was like death. It was miserable.

Scott never had to deal with pregnancy in his primary family. He was the youngest and he liked it that way. Who wants to deal with the competition of another child, anyway? His mother never made him do that; neither should Laci. After all, he was his mother's son. Jackie Peterson was no stranger to problems and controversy. She had a difficult life and had given away a few children for adoption. We don't know the impact of Jackie's choices on her son's behavior, but it would not be much of a stretch to say that Scott got the idea from Jackie that you get rid of anyone you don't want in your life.

Messages in families can be communicated in all kinds of ways, in some cases on an unconscious level. Modern psychoanalysts believe that a person's basic sense of himself predates cognitive and verbal abilities, and hence even surpasses the subjective sense of self. Once established, this basic identity is lifelong.

On some unconscious level did Scott believe that unwanted individuals should be disposed of? That there was no place for them? Perhaps this is where Amber Frey came in. She was more like his mother Jackie: She already had a child. Scott could idealize her and imagine that she would not ask him to give up his childlike status. He could even be easily and effortlessly Amber's knight in shining armor, like his dad was to his mom.

Of course Amber Frey was by no means perfect—she had her share of hard knocks in the world. She was lonely and had a history of looking for love in all the wrong places. Scott was not the first married man she had been involved with. In fact, the man she was involved with prior to Scott was also expecting a child with his pregnant wife. It seemed Amber had a propensity for dating men with pregnant wives. That being the case, it still seems that when she met Scott, Amber was trying to make better social choices for herself. Scott presented himself to Amber as the romantic ideal. His charming and glib words were used to assuage the pain he felt he would ultimately cause in his relationships. As this always worked for him in the past, he had no reason to think that it would not work for him now.

Yet it was Amber who sealed Scott's fate during the trial. Their taped phone conversations showed how easily and effortlessly Scott could lie. And his lies were elaborate. In some of the phone calls he sounded weak and pathetic. It was not difficult to imagine that his relationship with Laci paralleled that with Amber Frey.

People who have poor impulse control are also more likely to have multiple affairs. Scott's relationship with Laci was filled with too much responsibility and reality. It was a drag. With Amber, however, Scott could be anyone, not unlike his role in his primary family. There was a "high" to the affair that helped him escape the pressures of his daily married life. The eventual problem with this new fantasy relationship was that Scott actually expected it to work out. During his affair with Amber his feelings of bitterness and recrimination toward his wife and unborn son increased. And yet Amber was ultimately victimized by Scott, just like Laci was.

Scott's life was all about him and his pleasure. His purchases underscored this point: the boat, the motorcycle, the pickup truck, all were impulsive, pleasure, id, and phallic purchases. He felt easily intruded on by others, especially when he found them too demanding. For a while, Laci allowed him to buy whatever he wanted, but that all changed when she became pregnant with their first child. Her maternal instinct intensified and Scott felt the pressure and the heat. All his past sexual indiscretions were no longer acceptable to Laci. She knew her husband was desirable to women and that he had a roving eye. She had protected him in the past when she found out about his affairs. She did not even tell her closest confidante—her mother—about them. She did not want to present Scott in a poor light and furthermore, she wanted to protect herself from hearing what she didn't want to hear, that she had married a cad.

Laci knew her husband's cheating signs. She was seeing them again, and she eventually confronted Scott. She had expected more from him, especially with the birth of their first child right around the corner. Enough was enough, and she put her foot down, which seemed to Scott like harassment. He was not going to let her stop him from being free. Scott's background had not prepared him to manage frustration.

Laci became like one big "no" to Scott. As discussed earlier, Scott's own parents had not said no to him; he surely was not going to let Laci say it now. Worse still, he knew this time she meant it, especially with the baby on the way, which was going to change everything soon anyway. Suddenly Scott felt that he had been bullied and pushed around long enough. That was it: It was either going to be Laci or Scott, and in true Scott Peterson fashion, he chose himself.

All he could think about was getting his freedom and his life back from Laci. In the heat of a moment of uncontrollable anger and rage, Laci was dead.

Scott didn't really mean to kill Laci. And since he didn't really mean it, he shouldn't have to pay with his life. He believed that if he got rid of Laci's body, it would be as if the murder had not really occurred. If he denied it hard enough, it would be as if he hadn't really killed her. He had always gotten away with things in the past, so there was no reason to think this time would be any different. He knew his parents would believe him anyway. They would support him.

They always did.

BRIAN TRIMBLE was another man who didn't want to hear no.

When police arrived at his suburban Harrisburg, Pennsylvania, home on January 10, 2003, they found his wife, Randi, twenty-seven, lying dead in the garage. She had been stabbed twenty-eight times. The house had been ransacked, and her husband Brian, twenty-seven, had discovered his wife's body upon returning home after a night of dinner and shopping with a friend. He had even saved all his receipts.

But police became suspicious of Brian almost immediately. The "ransacking" appeared staged, with items tossed throughout the house as if the idea was to make a mess rather than steal anything. More important, some valuables were apparently missing while others, like everything in Brian's computer room, were untouched. In addition, the only open window in the house was too small for a burglar to get through, while the front door was unlocked, suggesting that Randi knew her attacker.

Randi was a speech language pathologist at Hershey Medical Center who worked extra hours to build a nest egg to help with the eventual care of Brian, who suffered from multiple sclerosis. The couple married in 2000 and Randi went into the marriage fully aware of Brian's condition and fate. While Randi sought to save her hard-earned money, Brian had other ideas.

He had a friend, Blaine Norris, twenty-five, a former Eagle Scout, high school honor student, and budding film director who was looking to produce a horror movie. The two men worked together as computer technicians for a local health insurance company, and Brian wanted to use some of Randi's money to buy video equipment for his friend's movie. But Randi said no, saying she wasn't going to give or lend money to someone she didn't know well. She also had other, more important designs on her money.

The couple argued over Randi's decision, but she wouldn't budge, adding tension to their already stressed marriage. The couple argued often, with Brian telling a coworker that he and his wife couldn't stand each other for long periods of time and they "couldn't even be in the same room together."

When he told his friend of his marital problems, Norris replied, "You know, I could take care of that for you."

Norris was joking, but Brian was furious with his wife, and Norris's suggestive comment soon turned into a plan. Brian decided to kill his wife and collect on her $94,000 insurance policy and $25,000 she had saved in her bank account.

Brian promised Norris $20,000, and for the next two months, over breakfast and lunch, the two men hatched their plot, from solid alibis to staging a robbery. Brian even sent Norris a computer link for a how-to book for hit men. The afternoon of the murder, Norris parked his car two blocks away from the Trimble home, and was let inside by Brian. There Norris turned over furniture and clothing and took some valuables, including jewelry. Brian went out to dinner with a friend to establish his alibi while Norris hid in the house, waiting for Randi to return home from work.

The day before, Norris bought new clothes, including a camouflage mask, gloves, and boots. He was wearing this disguise when Randi finally walked in. Norris surprised her and first tried to strangle her with an electrical cord from a Christmas tree. But Randi fought back, placing her hand between the cord and her neck, and with her other hand she pulled the mask away which, to her surprise, revealed Norris to be her attacker. Norris then took out a knife as Randi begged for her life and then began to pray.

Given their initial theories, Cumberland County police believed there was but one suspect: Brian Trimble. But a detective with the East Pennsboro Township police, Richard "Chip" Dougherty, thought the crime scene looked like a "TV burglary," and decided there had to be a second person involved. Dougherty and another detective, Les Frehling, a twenty-five-year veteran, spent four months on their investigation, part of which included a wiretap on Brian's home phone.

Brian was initially unaware that he was a suspect, believing instead that he was aiding in the police investigation. He met with Detective Frehling two weeks after the murder, at which time he related the events of the day and told the detective what he found when he returned home. Brian didn't know that he was locking himself into a story that would later produce a list of inconsistencies. Detectives were also following a money trail of receipts from both Brian and Norris that clearly indicated their involvement.

While the police moved cautiously, assembling one piece of evidence after another (including wiretaps), Brian collected the insurance money and paid his friend the promised $20,000. He also purchased an Xbox, a television, and new furniture. Before Randi's funeral Brian even requested a refund on tickets for a planned cruise with his wife.

Toward the end of the investigation both Brian and Norris knew they were suspects. Detective Dougherty would show up unannounced at Brian's home, or during surveillance he'd make himself visible to the increasingly nervous pair. Norris reacted by sending an anonymous letter to the *Harrisburg Patriot-News* and a TV station, claiming to be a professional hit man from outside the area and listing the details of the murder.

Police finally brought Brian in and told him about their wiretaps, after which he confessed, linking Norris, who had told police he was at his girlfriend's house, to the killing. The detectives obtained a warrant to search Norris's car, where they found a receipt from a clothing store in Lancaster, where Norris had purchased a camouflage mask and other items, including a seven-inch knife, on January 9, 2003, the night before the murder. They also questioned his girlfriend, who told them that Norris was supposed to arrive at her home at 6:30 P.M. for dinner. He hadn't gotten there until 9 P.M. Randi Trimble had died around 8 P.M.

Norris was arrested and charged, along with Brian, for the murder of Randi Trimble.

Both men pled guilty and avoided trial. They are serving life terms.

FINANCES are often the top cause of arguments for married couples, especially newly married couples. Randi Trimble, a speech pathologist, appeared to be more levelheaded than her husband about managing household finances. She wanted to save for the future, and she was thoughtful and mature about where the family money should go. Brian, on the other hand, was more childlike and impulsive. He wanted what he wanted, when he wanted it, and he was not good at waiting. It was an issue that would ultimately turn out to be lethal.

On one occasion, Brian wanted to use some of the family money his wife had saved to buy video equipment for his friend's movie. When his wife said no and would not change her mind, he became enraged. Brian hated his wife for this. He did not want to be told no by anyone, especially Randi. He told his movie-making friend, Norris, about his recent marital problems and said that he could not stand his wife anymore. Norris told him he could "take care of" it for him, obviously meaning that he would kill her. One could argue that Norris blurred his reality life with his fantasy life. Killing his friend's wife would be like playing a part and directing his own horror movie, only this movie was real, fatally real.

There was also another element to this story: Brian had multiple sclerosis. While the disease eventually leaves its victims paralyzed before they die, the progression is highly variable, sometimes quick, other times lengthy. Randi knew about Brian's condition before they married, which makes their relationship particularly sad and hard to understand. Randi agreed to marry a man, knowing that one day their lives together would eventually become very difficult. This is a huge decision for any woman to make, particularly one so young.

A speech therapist, Randi was maternal and nurturing by nature. She was able to use her head and her heart when it came to making decisions about her life. She loved Brian enough to take on his future health challenges. If anyone could do it, she felt she could. She was the exact opposite of her husband. For Brian, living in the moment was the priority and he was focused on the here and now. And anyone who got in his way needed to watch out. When Randi said no to him about something he really wanted, she became no different than his MS, the disease that would ultimately stifle his independence and take his life.

That was one of the reasons that Brian lashed out. After all, Randi knew he was living on borrowed time, and she wasn't the victim of a horrible disease. She should be more compassionate. How could she always be thinking about the future when he did not really have a future? The future meant nothing to him. In fact, it was downright unpleasant and depressing to think about it. There was nothing in it for him except for wheelchairs, adult diapers, and drooling all over himself. His future was bleak and Randi, of all people, knew it. What was his wife thinking? She was just being overbearing and thinking about herself. After all, she didn't have to worry about her future. She could save to her heart's content because she had a future to enjoy, to fantasize and feel hopeful about. He did not. His joys, fantasies, and dreams were available to him only in the moment, and only for as long as his body could hold out. His friend Blaine Norris understood his reality, why didn't his wife?

Thus, Randi became more of a burden than an asset. When Brian first married her, he thought they could enjoy a nice relationship and that Randi would let him have whatever he wanted. At least, that is the way it seemed when they first dated. In the beginning there wasn't anything she wouldn't do for him. He loved that and had grown to expect it. But things had changed since they got married and this infuriated him. He did not know how long he would have before his disease ravaged his body and ultimately took over his life. He did not need a wife to do the same thing.

If Randi was not going to add to his life and make life easier for him, she would have to go. He was going to have what he wanted whether his wife liked it or not. Brian was depressed and angry. He felt after all he had been through in life he deserved a little joy and pleasure. He thought he could get that with his wife Randi, but obviously he had made a mistake. She was a ball and chain and he would be better off without her. The insurance money from her death would only secure the freedom he had longed for and was entitled to. He had earned it. He already had one ball and chain in his life, the MS. He did not need another. With Blaine Norris's generous offer, he could finally have it all.

As discussed earlier in this chapter, we tend to associate

temper tantrums with toddlers. Infants and toddlers experience a lot of frustration in their lives because of the wide discrepancy between what they want to do and what they are able to do. Because kids are small, these outbursts are more of a nuisance than a danger.

Dealing effectively with temper tantrums in adults is about learning how to exercise self-control. Self-control is critical if you want to get along with people and succeed in life. It requires thinking before acting. If left uncontrolled impulsive behavior can have negative or even dangerous consequences, as it did for Brian and Randi.

Brian reacted to his wife like an oppositional child or adolescent rebelling against a problematic or restrictive parent. This rebellious dynamic produced an intense and overwhelming anger that would not wane over time. Brian could not resolve his chronic and aversive emotional reaction. He was ruminating, and during this period of rumination his impulsive and explosive rage got the best of him. He thought the only way to escape his wife's unswayable decision was to have her eliminated. Once Randi was out of the way, he could have what he wanted and was entitled to. He was just safeguarding his right to a life.

Brian's act was not only highly reactive, it was cowardly. Not unlike Rabbi Neulander, he hired someone to do the killing. The relationship between Brian and Norris was pathological and perverse. Norris killed Randi with such a degree of rage. The contact was up close and appeared to be personal. One wonders if he had killed like this before. And what were Norris's real feelings toward Brian?

Brian liked people who would do anything for him. He thought Randi would do anything until she showed him otherwise. Brian would favor the person who best met his needs. It was all about expedience. Whoever did not cooperate would be disposed of. Brian was excited by Norris's willingness to do anything. Norris's approach to life exhilarated Brian, perhaps because Brian already felt dead and something about being around Norris helped him to vicariously feel more powerful and alive. So he went with the person who gave him the exciting feeling he wanted to have in life, and went against the one person who had supported him the most.

8

The Transference Killer

TRANSFERENCE is a subject generally reserved to psychologically oriented or therapeutic circles. It is a reenactment of a person's early life experiences, impulses, and fantasies. The individual replaces a protagonist from his past with a current partner from the present. For example, a wife's behavior may remind a husband of his irritating or abusive mother. Thus, transference is a misrepresentation of the present. The individual sees what he needs to see, rather than what is there.

In an intimate-partner homicide, the person from the past gets superimposed onto the current spouse. Unless appropriately analyzed, this transference of old feelings onto the spouse is hard to distinguish. The bad "mother" from the past becomes no different from the bad spouse in the moment. The nature of transference is based in unfulfilled emotional needs from childhood. According to some research, there are striking similarities in certain behaviors between the mother/infant interaction and that of romantic lovers. The similarities include close proximity, hugging, kissing, touching, and performing distinctive gestures.

The emotional and physical language of love is learned very early in life. When we fall in love, we draw more or less from our experiences with our early caretakers. The emotional instinct or desire of the person in love is ultimately to become a baby and to be completely indulged with love. But even in the most secure situations, a caretaker can frustrate the baby. There are always obstacles to experiencing love. In the most extreme cases the obstacles result from negligence, abandonment, abuse, loss of love, or symptoms of a parent's psychopathology. In adulthood, we often choose partners who remind us of our parents. We choose them in part to help re-create our childhood struggles in order to help us resolve the original trauma and move on. In some cases the original trauma is so hateful and damaging that the partner who re-creates it ends up being violent or murderous.

With this in mind, individuals select a partner who fit their idea or model of someone they can relate to in the same way they related to a parent or other family member. They can even distort the love object and see him/her as more like this significant person from the past than he/she really is. If this distortion does not happen naturally, the transference killer's personality is capable of provoking his romantic partner into the behavior that he seeks. All of these tendencies make it less likely that such personalities will be able to achieve the intimacy and/or "fantasy bond" they are searching for. The anger and rage that comes from this realization can lead certain individuals to commit murder or violence against their partner.

And small differences can sometimes cause great problems. In many couples, one spouse is seen as the potentially good parent. People who can't bear the thought or idea that good and bad can exist within the same person can feel depressed, anxious, and sometimes murderous. When feelings of humiliation or degradation increase to the point that a person feels worthless or hates himself, resulting suicidal feelings can trigger homicidal actions.

Freud had a basically pessimistic view of love. He said that violence is hardly surprising or exceptional in interpersonal relationships: "The evidence of psycho-analysis shows that almost every emotional relation between two people which lasts for some time—marriage, friendship, the relationships between parents and children—leaves a sediment of feelings of aversion and hostility, which only escapes perception as a result of repression."

The transference killer is unable to repress this hostility, and for MICHAEL PETERSON, it was déjà vu all over again.

Peterson, fifty-nine, was a novelist and onetime newspaper columnist who often infuriated local police with his blistering attacks on their competence. But on December 9, 2001, it was Peterson who called police during the early morning hours to report that his wife Kathleen, forty-eight, was bleeding and unconscious. When police arrived at the Petersons' expansive Durham, North Carolina, home, Kathleen was dead.

Michael claimed his wife had fallen down the stairs and struck her head. Investigators didn't believe him. They found blood on cabinetry in the kitchen, and the amount of blood pooled around Kathleen's head seemed like far too much to have come from a simple fall. And it seemed equally unlikely that such a fall could have caused all of Kathleen's head wounds. The medical examiner also concluded the damage to Kathleen's neck indicated that someone had tried to strangle her.

Within a week Peterson was arrested and charged with murdering his wife. The reason, police later said, was that Peterson was angered that his wife had racked up over $100,000 in credit card debt, and he wanted to collect on her $1.4 million insurance policy. After Peterson was released on $850,000 bond, investigators received another tantalizing piece of information: In 1985, another woman who knew Peterson had been found dead at the bottom of a stairway—that time in Germany, where Peterson then lived.

The woman, Elizabeth Ratliff, was a next-door neighbor and friend who, like Kathleen, had suffered head wounds. Though local authorities had ruled her death accidental, there were too many similarities for prosecutors to dismiss. And under North Carolina rules of evidence, the prosecutors could use Ratliff's death as a comparison.

Peterson denied having any part in Ratliff's death, and pointed to her two daughters, who he subsequently raised as evidence of his love and loyalty to her. As for Kathleen, Peterson claimed his wife had been drinking when she fell down the stairs, hitting her head. He said that she was bleeding but still conscious and that she had tried to get up but slipped on her own blood and fell to the floor, striking her head a second time. His defense appeared preposterous, but friends said the pair had a loving relationship and murder was not something anyone could even consider.

PETERSON grew up in a military family, moving from base to base, country to country. He attended Duke University, studying political science and editing the student newspaper. Writing had always intrigued Peterson, who thought of himself as a successor to Hemingway. After graduating in 1965 he was hired by the U.S. Department of Defense to research and write papers supporting the war in Vietnam. Peterson decided to enlist in the Marines in 1967 and told friends he had been in combat, which led to injuries and a Purple Heart.

Following his discharge four years later, Peterson served as a government consultant. He married his first wife, Patricia, and the couple had two sons. By the mid-1980s they were living in Germany and it was there that, in 1985, their next-door neighbor Elizabeth Ratliff was found dead. Ratliff was a widow and mother of two daughters. She had worked as a schoolteacher for the Department of Defense. The night before she died, Ratliff had dinner with Peterson and his wife, after which Peterson walked Ratliff home. She had several lacerations to the head and her death was ruled the result of a brain hemorrhage.

The Petersons later returned to North Carolina, raising their two sons and Ratliff's two daughters. Peterson began writing and authored three semi-successful novels, all based on his military experience. The money earned from his books went into the purchase of an 11,000-square-foot home. He also served as a columnist for the local newspaper, the *Durham Herald-Sun.*

Peterson was still married when he met Kathleen Atwater. She was ten years younger and, like Peterson, had graduated from Duke, in her case with an engineering degree. Kathleen had become a successful executive earning $140,000 per year. Peterson divorced Patricia and in 1997 married Kathleen. It was the second marriage for Kathleen, who had a daughter. Along with Peterson's two sons and Ratliff's two daughters, five children were then living in the Peterson home.

By all accounts Kathleen and Michael Peterson enjoyed each other, spending weekends at their home entertaining friends, often with plenty of alcohol. Kathleen continued to work while Peterson wrote. He also decided to run for mayor of Durham in 1999, but during the campaign he was forced to make an embarrassing public admission: the Purple Heart he received in Vietnam was not awarded for wounds received in combat, but from an auto accident in Japan.

Peterson lost the election and returned to his writing. Perhaps his greatest story was the one he told on the night of Kathleen's death when the police arrived at his home. Peterson, wearing shorts, was covered in blood. The medical examiner later concluded that Kathleen died from "blunt force trauma" to the head and that her injuries were inconsistent with a fall. Peterson was subsequently arrested. After investigators learned of Ratliff's death some 16 years earlier, they had her body exhumed from her grave in Texas and brought to North Carolina, where pathologists concluded that she had not died from natural causes, but like Kathleen Peterson, from "blunt force trauma," and from assault from seven separate blows to the head. In addition, as stated in the original police report, a witness had seen Peterson "running" from Ratliff's home that night in 1985.

Following a lengthy trial in October 2002, Michael Peterson was found guilty of murdering Kathleen and sentenced to life in prison. He was later charged with the 1985 murder of Elizabeth Ratliff and is awaiting trial.

One of the reasons this case is so fascinating is the repeat performance of the killing that occurred sixteen years before. After an evening with Peterson and his first wife, Elizabeth Ratliff had also ended up dead at the bottom of her staircase. Ratliff and Kathleen Peterson would never have a chance to meet, but their deaths were not the only thing they had in common: they eerily resembled each other. The two could have been twins separated at birth. Perhaps Michael fell so quickly for Kathleen because she reminded him of Elizabeth Ratliff. For Peterson, marrying Kathleen was a second chance to make things right, and his motives were born from transference, where one person gets substituted for another and is experienced in the same way.

The ideas we have about ourselves and those around us are influenced by our original caregivers and early life experiences. If we are routinely criticized or put down, we can develop a damaged sense of ourselves and self-worth. When we are young, we see our parents as all-powerful and the center of our universe. If they view us as bad we automatically assume they are correct. We internalize their negative feelings and ideas about us, making these feelings part of our own self-view.

When a child suffers from a harmful childhood experience, even if it is not remembered consciously, it can create emotional scars and inhibit that child's ability to develop close and rewarding relationships with the people in his or her adult life.

The attachment styles that we develop in childhood stay with us for a lifetime. They influence everything from our feelings of security to our ability to develop healthy intimacy with others. If we develop a healthy attachment style we have a better chance for trusting, rewarding, and loving relationships with others. If our primary childhood caregivers were unavailable, critical, indifferent, and unsupportive, we may be unable to later rely on others for love.

We are biologically designed to seek and maintain attachment to others in part to learn the lessons of love and trust. When people enter into a marital relationship, both will bring with them their past unresolved conflicts, expectations, suspicions, and upsets. There is a strong propensity to want to recreate neglectful, abusive, and hurtful childhood relationships with our adult partners in an attempt to resolve old psychic wounds. A trigger in the current relationship can unleash the old feelings and reactions, in turn creating confusion between what is an old hurt and what is a new one.

It's probable that Peterson replayed something with these two women that originated with one or both of his parents. Who might these two women have brought to his mind? Michael Peterson's sister was one of the most vocal family members at his trial to state her feeling about her brother's guilt. It is very possible that she knew something about her brother that the two victims never did.

It appears that Michael developed an attraction toward the

first woman, Elizabeth Ratliff. It's possible that he may have killed her accidentally, felt remorseful, and in an attempt to undo his wrong, devoted himself to raising her two children.

Why would he commit the two murders in the same way? One answer could be because he got away with it the first time, he thought he could get away with it the second time. He might have been compelled by earlier experience to repeat this pattern of homicidal violence. He could have killed Elizabeth accidentally in a moment of rage and by the time he was married for the second time, his rage may have become habitual. It is also possible that Kathleen became enraged with her husband on that fateful night and confronted him about the bills, his lack of professional success, and about an alleged online gay dalliance. She could have been drinking, paranoid, and asking him multiple questions that drove him crazy. He felt assaulted by Kathleen and her intense desire to meet her needs, which were conflicting with his needs, which made him feel threatened and out of control. In his mind, Kathleen was just like all of the other women in his life who had failed him. She was like Elizabeth. They all became one person linked and merged together. By the time he regained control of himself, Kathleen was dead. It was just like what happened with Elizabeth all over again.

The convincing 911 call could be attributed to Michael's novelistic skills. Fiction writers commonly imagine feelings one might have in a particular situation, including murder. He might have asked himself, How would a hysterical husband act after finding out his beloved wife was dead?

The panic Michael Peterson felt could be attributed to what the police were likely to dig up about his past and how suspect his background would make him look. Certainly he would not want the police to find out about the previous dead woman in his life, his mounting debt, and the gay escort he was having a dalliance with prior to his wife's death. Maybe Peterson viewed the police department as one big floating superego, the part of the personality that punishes an individual for perceived and real wrongdoings. He may have attacked the police in his writing in an attempt to justify his behavior, or it could have been his guilty conscious trying to get caught. After all, if he made the police angry, would they not grow more anxious to prove his guilt?

We also take into account the impact of Vietnam. Although Michael Peterson saw little direct combat, any amount is bound to have a profound psychological and frightening affect. Michael Peterson also wrote about war, so it would not be unreasonable to suggest that his military experience affected him. *The Journal of Traumatic Stress* theorizes that war-zone stressors could increase the severity of later intimate-partner violence. The more threatened an individual felt in combat, the more likely he is to suffer from post-traumatic stress. Overall, the journal reported that a veteran's background, including his history of trauma, and PTSD symptomatology, contribute significantly to the risk of initiating violence against his partner.

Interestingly, a veteran's poor relationship with his mother, even more so than with his father, appears to be a major predictor of intimate-partner violence. Michael Peterson expected way too much from the women in his life, and in a moment of stress, when they disappointed and enraged him, he could not help but feel annihilated, threatened, and at war with them. The women in his life all became one and the same: his enemy. In an attempt to protect himself he went into a mode that left these women dead.

CELESTE BEARD could not be pleased with the man in her life.

During the early morning hours of October 2, 1999, her

husband Steven Beard, a Texas millionaire, was awakened by a sudden blow to his stomach followed by searing pain.

Unsure of what happened, he immediately called 911 and told emergency operators that his guts had "jumped out of my stomach." When paramedics arrived at Beard's estate in Austin, the doors were locked, so they broke through a sliding glass door. After they rushed to Steven's upstairs bedroom, they were met with a ghastly sight: Beard, seventy-four, lying in a blood-soaked bed, his stomach blown apart. Nearby was a .20 gauge shotgun shell.

Beard was taken to the hospital, where he clung to life for four months before succumbing to his wound. He left behind an estate valued at $10 million. While in the hospital, police focused their investigation on Steven's wife, Celeste, thirty-seven. The couple had met at a local country club, where Celeste worked as a waitress. She was a widow and the mother of twin teenage daughters. Her first husband had committed suicide.

When they met, Steven was a widower still trying to cope with the loss of his wife of forty-five years. He was a media mogul and part owner of a local television station, and he was immediately smitten with the younger Celeste. They began to date, and Steven showered Celeste with gifts, including fine jewelry. He eventually asked her to move in with him. For Celeste, whose life had been filled with hardship and debt, it was a dream come true.

They married in 1994, and three years later Steven officially adopted Celeste's daughters. Celeste was living out a fairy tale, complete with exotic vacations, multiple homes, and, of course, plenty of money.

But just six days after the shooting, investigators made a startling arrest. Celeste had a friend, Tracey Tarlton, who owned a shotgun, and police matched the shell casing found in Steven's bedroom to Tarlton's gun.

Celeste and Tracey had known each other just a few months, meeting when both were patients at a psychiatric hospital in Austin. Celeste had been admitted suffering from severe depression, a condition she had battled for her entire life, having been raised in a deeply troubled home, where she claims to have been sexually abused. At one time, Celeste had tried to slit her wrists.

Tarlton, a bookstore manager, had her own mental issues. According to police she was bipolar and heard voices that implored her to commit suicide. She was dependent on drugs and also suffered from depression. The two women struck up a friendship and remained in touch after they were discharged from the hospital. They soon became lovers. Following her arrest, Tarlton initially protected her friend. But a year later she learned that Celeste had remarried, meeting her new husband at a bar and moving with him to Fort Worth. Tarlton realized that Celeste was moving on with her life. And it was Celeste, Tarlton reasoned, who had manipulated her into killing Steven Beard.

Just days before her own murder trial was scheduled to begin, Tarlton agreed to a plea deal. She would receive a jail term of twenty years and in return would implicate Celeste in the murder of her husband, claiming they were lesbian lovers and it was Celeste who was behind her husband's murder, hoping to collect his $10 million estate. Tarlton claimed that Celeste had complained bitterly about her husband and his abusive ways and that they had tried on several occasions to kill Steven, once by suffocation.

Celeste vehemently denied the charges, but she was subsequently indicted.

During the sensational trial in 2004, prosecutors brought out witness after witness who testified to Celeste's duplicity and desire to get rid of her aging husband. Included on the witness list were Celeste's twin daughters, who testified that their mother wished Steven would just "die." They also told of seeing their mother put sleeping pills in Steven's food, then leaving the home to meet secretly with Tarlton, whom they believed to be a lesbian. Other witnesses told of the affection displayed between Celeste and Tarlton, and prosecutors claimed that Celeste used Tarlton's emotions against her, manipulating her to kill Steven.

Tarlton provided the most telling testimony, stating that Celeste had been disgusted with her husband, from his appearance to his age, and maintained that she couldn't take him anymore and would kill herself if she had to stay with him. Believing she was protecting her friend and lover, Tarlton shot Steven.

Celeste's attorney, Dick DeGuerrin, sought to prove that Tarlton alone had devised the plan to kill Steven. But the jury was swayed by Tarlton's testimony and the testimony of others, including Celeste's daughters, and found Celeste guilty of murder. She was sentenced to life in prison.

UNLIKE Michael Peterson, who seemed to be more hopeful when he entered into his romantic relationships, Celeste Beard Johnson was too angry to be hopeful. She began relationships with a spirit of retaliation and a sadistic vengeance. She transferred her original set of hateful feelings toward both her parents onto her current relationships with the intimates in her life. Celeste Beard Johnson's background shows how a disturbed childhood can contribute to murderous impulses and tendencies.

Celeste was adopted into a very dysfunctional family. Her parents, Edwin and Nancy Johnson, were not well matched; in fact, some people found them to be quite an odd mix. After six years of marriage and several miscarriages, the Johnsons adopted four children in under four years. Celeste was the oldest girl and second oldest of the four. She was curious about her birth parents and would often ask Nancy for her adoption papers, but Nancy refused to show them. When Celeste's older brother Cole asked for the papers on his real family, Nancy declined and angrily told her son he was the offspring of a prostitute and wife beater who was born only because his birth mother was paid not to have an abortion. Nancy also told her adopted children that their "real" mothers didn't want them and neither did she. Cole later described her as brutal when angry.

Life quickly deteriorated when Edwin lost his job and Nancy was hospitalized for depression in a local psychiatric ward. Cole remembered the children were often scared by their mother's erratic and dangerous behavior, which included holding their heads under water. Later, Nancy said she thought she was washing away her children's sins.

Celeste was described as playful and cute and the one child best able to charm her parents. But both her brothers also remembered her dark side. They describe her as frightening and calculating. One minute she would do anything for you and the next would be horribly mean and manipulative. She also instigated fights among her siblings. As the years went by, Celeste displayed signs of being deeply troubled. She suffered through nightmares so violent that they precluded her from getting braces because she clenched her teeth so tightly at night. After her adoptive father lost his job he became angry, disheveled, and bizarre, and the financial strain contributed to the obvious marital troubles.

Celeste had a particularly hard time coping, in part due to her friendship with a schoolmate. The friend lived in a nice home with a happy, well off, and loving family. The friend's parents would often buy the young Celeste expensive gifts and take her on trips. Having money became associated in Celeste's mind with being healthy, well taken care of, loved, and secure. She experienced the good life and wanted this kind of life for herself.

Celeste's parents eventually divorced; it was bitter and

brutal, and no family member was lucky enough to escape the venomous war that ensued. Cole described his father as crazy, referring to himself as Jedediah. And Nancy was especially vicious, brainwashing her daughters to hate their father. Celeste would later testify against her father, claiming he had sexually molested her. She also accused him of having tried to kill her. By the time Celeste turned fourteen, her intense rage and anger was already obvious to everyone who knew her. Her wild teens led her into an early chaotic marriage and she gave birth to her twin daughters at the young age of eighteen.

A person's childhood experience of abuse or abandonment can be so horrifying that he or she experiences the normal response to emotional weakness as life-threatening. Needing and trusting can be hurtful and painful. When women feel this way, they are more likely to use violence to try to control and diminish their mates in order to feel safe with them. They will do anything to avoid feeling that they are the weaker of the pair. According to psychoanalyst Jessica Benjamin in her book *The Bonds of Love,* the need to dominate is an attempt to deny dependency. Celeste went into her adult world vowing never to be the victim of the kind of abuse she had previously experienced.

Love gone wrong can shatter children and make them into damaged adults—fragile, hateful, and fearful. For people like Celeste Beard Johnson, who had been physically and psychologically wounded by "love," the need to retaliate carried into her future relationships. In some circles transference is occasionally called shadowboxing. The ghosts of the past that one is reacting to are not the person who is currently standing before her. All of these ghosts get rolled into one person, who is experienced in the same way. Unfortunately, it is often the innocent person who pays with his life in this kind of romantic scenario. The attacker is attacking a symbolic target. The targets, in Celeste's case, were both male and female.

In the case of *Texas* vs. *Celeste Beard Johnson,* Celeste had simultaneously attacked two of her lovers, Steven Beard and Tracey Tarlton. They both represented the original caretakers who'd failed her, first her birth parents and then later her adoptive parents. She was getting rid of people based on her rage against a remembered trauma, the trauma of being rejected and not taken care of properly. Taking Steven's money and manipulating and pretending to love people when she did not was just another way to hurt people who failed her. Celeste's symbolic targets were anyone who loved her and/or wanted something from her. It was all about her. At least that is the way she wanted it to be.

Celeste was a woman who was incapable of loving anyone. Women who have a disturbed early background are more likely to feel violent and act violent toward others because they have not been able to come to terms with adult situations such as maternal loss, parental violence, or a mother who is not able to meet their needs. This makes these women more likely to have an unplanned pregnancy in adolescence, to develop depression in adulthood, to be victimized in intimate relationships, and to be disadvantaged in terms of alternative or escape solutions from abusive relationships—since through their own experience in abusive relationships they have developed a learned helplessness.

For Celeste, her pain became other people's pain. She reenacted what had been done to her: seduce, possess, and then reject and/or eliminate. Only then could she feel like she had some control in her life. And since she really hated all people she was incapable of human intimacy—due to her intolerant feelings of fear, love, vulnerability, and intense anger. Handling these emotions correctly is fundamental to experiencing true love and meaningful connection.

Celeste Beard Johnson was a con artist who had a talent for finding and seducing vulnerable people. She despised people who were weak because they reminded her on some level of who she could never be. She had an inclination to hate any person who reminded her that he was not like her. In some cases adopted children suffer significant problems even when they are adopted by loving parents, which was certainly not the case for Celeste. So much rejection had resulted in a permanently wounded psyche.

Children who are adopted, even if they are loved, can feel like they do not fit in or belong to the family and they may develop an ambiguous or tenuous sense of attachment. It's not uncommon for them to feel that their birth parents have rejected them. Celeste experienced both, her birth parents as rejecting and her adopted parents as impaired, rejecting, and abusive. When this happens, it leads a person to see herself as damaged goods and to believe that she must have done something terrible in order to be sent away from her birth mother. There is often an accompanying feeling of shame that is interpreted by the child to mean that she was so bad that she had to be given away. The issue of control becomes crucial for such individuals because things have been done to them that they feel they had no choice in. They had no choice in ending up in the family that they did. Not knowing their birth family, they often struggle hard to find some sense of control in their lives.

Children who are adopted often feel overcontrolled by simple rules that are easily accepted by kids who are not adopted. Adoptees may displace rage toward the adopted parents that they really feel toward their birth parents. In Celeste's case, she felt rage toward both sets of parents. Later this rage transferred to just about anyone and everyone. Any feeling of rejection experienced by Celeste triggered her murderous rage.

This rage was directed toward anyone who did not give her

what she wanted, or withheld from her or disappointed her. In turn she was prompted to relive the feelings of murderous hatred that she experienced for the people in her life who had first rejected her—a transformation called traumatic reenactment. All of these people merge into one person (her husbands, her daughters, her lovers—basically everyone in her life). She threatens suicide as a manipulative ploy. Celeste could be fighting an underlying impulse to kill herself, and in an attempt to defend against it (or not feel it), she becomes ferocious and murderous to the people around her. Who did Steve Beard represent to her? She viewed him as a man who constricted her control over her own life.

Both Steve and Tracey were vulnerable when they met Celeste. Steve was a grieving widower and Tracey was a mentally ill, romantic obsessive, who had just been hospitalized. Celeste's emotional zone was limited. She was either at a rest/calm state or in a state of rage. There were not a lot of subtleties in her emotional repertoire. This type of person can easily go into a homicidal frenzy when angered.

Celeste had some type of fantasy in her head of what Steve should be or should have done for her after she married him. He clearly did not live up to her fantasy. She felt extremely entitled and that all of his money was in fact hers. Without a broad range of feelings it does not matter if you are alive or dead. The only thing that matters is getting rid of the annoyance and the discomfort. Celeste did not have mature problem-solving skills. She just wanted to eliminate anyone who got in her way. It was her for her. The incest and abuse she had experienced could have contributed to her reasons for marrying Steve Beard. He was old enough to be her father. She might have married him as a way to have legitimate sex with her "father" instead of incestuous sex. But the marriage may have helped her to reexperience the murderous feelings she had toward her father.

I had a chance to meet and talk with Celeste's two daughters during a *Catherine Crier Live* show on Court TV. They were decent girls who adored Steve Beard and considered him a loving adoptive father. They were deeply saddened by his death and remain close with the Beard family to this day. They also loved their biological father, whom they considered a loving man who had taken good care of them until his suicide. It is interesting to see that children, despite being genetically linked to their parents, can still be so constitutionally unlike them. Celeste Beard's girls were nothing like her. They wanted to connect and to make something out of themselves and their lives. But in Celeste's world, even her daughters weren't safe, since their mother could not experience them as separate human beings. They were useful to her only if she could see them as extensions of herself. Once she couldn't, she threatened to get rid of them, too.

9
The Revenge Killer

MANY murders are motivated by revenge, a very common yet noxious desire for retribution.

Although revenge is frequently discussed in this book, the revenge killer's motivation is leveling the score. For example, while some revenge murders are spontaneous, many are carried out with calm and precision. By nature, the revenge killer is a victim of his/her own emotions. Lacking the ability to handle negative emotions often leads to an overpowering sense of abandonment or rejection. Yet, unlike the average person who seeks help from the outside, the revenge killer remains tormented. It should be noted that many revenge killers have endured long-term abuse—be it verbal, sexual, and/or physical. Interestingly, while this perpetrator is unable to deal with an emotional crisis, he is very capable of organizing an attack. In such cases, the individual has reached a point where his emotions are insufferably disordered and torturous. A solution is found by pathologically attempting to regain some measure of control, and usually, murder is the *only* answer.

SUSAN WRIGHT was a twenty-seven-year-old stay-at-home mother of two young children. She was blond and attractive, a former waitress and topless dancer. She met her husband, Jeff, thirty-two, a carpet salesman, in 1997 on a beach in Galveston, Texas. Eight months pregnant when they married, Susan was looking forward to a happy life, given her husband's enthusiasm for a warm home and healthy family. But Jeff was also demanding, and as the years passed, Susan developed an uncanny level of perfectionism. She cooked and cleaned with neurotic precision, and dinner was *always* on time for her husband.

Until one day when she decided to stop.

ON January 18, 2003, Jeff Wright's body was discovered in a shallow grave in the backyard of the Wrights' suburban Houston home. He had been stabbed 193 times.

Prior to the discovery of the body, Susan told friends that the couple had an argument and Jeff had walked out. It was only *after* Jeff had been missing for nearly a week and was subsequently fired from his job that Susan came forth, via an attorney, claiming to have killed him. Susan argued that her husband returned home that night from a boxing lesson in a drug-induced state and slapped their son, Bradley. When she confronted Jeff, he became enraged and dragged her to the bedroom where he raped her and threatened her with a knife. Susan claimed she kicked Jeff in the groin, retrieved the knife, and stabbed him repeatedly, saying she couldn't stop because she feared he would steal the knife back and kill her.

It was the end, she said, of a relationship that had soured

soon after their son was born. Jeff, she said, became more controlling, even becoming abusive and violent when she failed to fulfill his wishes. Her life with Jeff, she said, was a living hell filled with constant beatings and mental torture. If she was late returning home from the store or her parents' home, he would accuse her of cheating.

Susan's family supported her claims of beatings and mental torture when the case went to trial in March 2004. Susan's sister testified that she had intervened during one of the couple's argument, bringing Susan and the two children to her home, where they spent one night before returning to Jeff. Susan's mother testified that she had seen her daughter with blackened eyes, and Susan claimed that her husband's temper would worsen when he did drugs. Indeed, the night Jeff was killed he had cocaine in his system. He was also unfaithful, she argued, and many of his girlfriends called their home. Worse still, Susan alleged that she had contracted herpes from him. Their marriage, said her attorney, was a "brutal, terrifying, sadistic relationship that spanned years" and Susan had to "kill or be killed." Jeff died, Susan said, because she "didn't want to die."

Prosecutors, however, had a different version of the events that led up to Jeff's death and pointed to evidence indicating his murder was calculated. They portrayed Jeff as a charming man who loved his family; an all-around good guy well liked by neighbors and coworkers. Friends testified that Susan and Jeff's relationship was something out of *Ozzie and Harriet*. In effect, the prosecution's case centered on the idea that Susan tied her husband to the bedpost with the promise of a romantic evening before killing him—all to gain his $200,000 life insurance. To prove their point, they said that after Susan stabbed her husband over and over and over again, she dragged his body to a makeshift pit in their backyard and buried him to hide the evidence. As for the extreme number of knife wounds, prosecutors argued that Susan rested at times before continuing. That, they said, gave her ample time to stop. Indeed, many of the 193 knife wounds were on the front, left side of his body, from the groin up to the face. She even stabbed him in the eye.

In the end, the jury believed the prosecution, and Susan Wright was found guilty of murder. She was sentenced to serve twenty-five years in prison.

IT is interesting that evidence was presented suggesting that Susan had grown up in an abusive household, with her mother suffering regular beatings at the hands of her father. During the trial, however, Susan's mother testified there had been no abuse, and the line of questioning ended. Later, however, during a network interview, Susan's sister, Cindy Stewart, a psychologist with a Ph.D., confirmed that the sisters repeatedly saw their mother abused by their father. The memory of the beatings, Cindy argued, lurked somewhere in Susan's mind and left an indelible imprint. From this vantage point, Cindy said, she could understand why Susan stabbed her husband 193 times.

"She stabbed Jeff for all the times that he punched her in the chest, and she stabbed him for all of the times that he raped her in the middle of the night. And she stabbed Jeff because he was just like her father."

Still, others argued that while Susan may have resented her husband for all the abuse heaped upon her, it was Jeff who secretly resented his wife, despite statements that the marriage had made him a "changed" man. As an example, during their whirlwind courtship, Susan told Jeff that she was taking birth control pills regularly, yet somehow she managed to get pregnant. Given that the pill is 99 percent effective, the most effective form of birth control on the market, Jeff couldn't help but think Susan had lied. Feeling both pressured and enraged, Jeff nonetheless decided to do the right thing, and with Susan eight months pregnant, they married.

Susan's depiction of her marriage spoke of a change in the couple's relationship soon after the birth of their first child, Bradley. Jeff proved to be a perfectionist and, in turn, became very demanding of his new wife. Susan claimed that he would fly off the handle when something was out of place, such as a few of the kids' toys strewn on the floor. For Jeff, if things were not exactly to his liking, anything could happen—and it usually wasn't good. Furthermore, there were problems arising from Jeff's drug dependence and his affairs with other women. Susan argued that such issues fueled episodes of rage, and it was she who was often the brunt of Jeff's impulsive brutality.

If you believe the prosecution's depiction, Susan had taken matters into her own hands using her own form of vigilante revenge. Her husband was not going to change, and if she wasn't going to get rid of him, who was? Some people choose spouses because unconsciously the same negative and familiar feelings they have about themselves are experienced with their spouses. This is called repetition compulsion. We gravitate toward the familiar in an attempt to fix it and make it better. Prosecutor Kelly Siegler told the jury that it was clear that Susan and her husband had an unhealthy marriage that was destined for failure, but she argued this conditions still could not explain the degree of rage behind Jeff's murder.

Behind her beautiful and seductive façade, Susan had an anger problem. While she and her husband allegedly had an abusive relationship, the severity of Jeff's wounds and the way in which she attacked him could not be justified as self-defense. Susan had never sought medical attention for her wounds and she had not suffered the characteristic bruising and broken bones typical of battered wives. The people around her were not aware of the severity of the situation. Instead, it appeared more likely that there had indeed been a desire to even up some perceived score and that revenge had been the probable motivation.

But let us rewind back to the moment of the crime.

According to the police, Susan was sick of the lies and sick of the abuse. She had a lot of time to think about her escape route, and murder appeared to be the best way for her to escape. After Jeff returned home from a hard day's work Susan knew exactly what she needed to do. Insisting that her husband never turned down a night of wild sex, after she put her two children to bed, she set the stage for the ultimate evening of sexual exhilaration. According to the prosecution's reconstruction of the evening, there were flickering candles carefully placed around the bedroom and to further set the mood, Susan dripped hot red wax all over her husband's excited body: first on his thigh, then on his genitals. There was even some left over for his buttocks.

Once the sex commenced, it was argued that Jeff was completely lost in his own desires. Susan was in the power seat now, and she coyly talked him into allowing her to tie him to the bedposts: first his left arm, then his right, and then finally his legs. Before Jeff realized what was happening, Susan pulled out a knife. Coolly and deliberately, she proceeded to stab him nearly two hundred times, from his head to his ankles. Many of the wounds came from directly on top of him, while others came from the side. There were superficial lacerations to the penis as well.

The logical interpretation here, as her sister Cindy argued, would be that Susan stabbed her husband in the penis for all the times he raped her, and in the leg for all the times he kicked her. One could also suggest that some of those 193 stab wounds were for all of the times Susan claimed her father beat her and her mother. Additionally, as we know, there was also evidence that Susan took a little break while on her vengeful rampage. This is particularly interesting. Why stop, pause, and then continue?

While we may never know with certainty, a good guess would be that she wanted to be certain her victim was dead. Fear plays a major role in abusive relationships, and Susan Wright's relationship was no exception. One could argue that by murdering her husband, Susan faced her greatest fear and defeated it.

After all was said and done she dragged her husband's lifeless and bloodied body into a shallow grave in the family's backyard. The murder weapon, a small hunting knife, was placed in a flowerpot on the patio. (The tip of the knife was later found in Jeffrey's brain.) Susan then cut the bedroom rug and bought bleach and paint to cover up the bloodstains. The bed frame, box spring, and bloodstained mattress were found partially disassembled and placed in the backyard. Receipts confirmed the purchase of the bleach, paint, and the potting soil used to ensure that the body was completely covered. Susan's revenge was complete.

ACCORDING to Dr. Phyllis Sharp, associate professor at Johns Hopkins School of Nursing, some women retaliate when they are hurt and victimized. Because they are often smaller in size than their abusers, they sometimes need to plan their escape in order to get out of a dangerous relationship. The legal system may penalize the abused woman for her careful planning, which can make her seem calculating and deceitful. But often such women have been abused for a very long time. The crimes against them may be no different from rape. "Under violent circumstances, you do whatever you need to, to survive," Dr. Sharp says. This phenomenon is also called battered women's syndrome, and murder under these conditions is sometimes used as a form of self-defense in reaction to severe mistreatment experienced throughout an abusive relationship. Could something unreasonable under normal circumstances be completely comprehensible considering the violent environment in which a battered individual lives? In other words, did Susan Wright really believe, at the moment of the crime, it was either kill or be killed?

Dr. Lenore Walker, who originally defined battered women's syndrome, says such women are unable to leave their abusers even when it seems to the outside world that they should. Over time, these women experience what is called a learned state of helplessness. They become dispirited and hopeless about their ability to leave or change their situation. Furthermore, Dr. Walker states that the battered woman exhibits "bizarre" behavior as a result of her victimization. So, a homicide committed by a victimized spouse can also be seen as a "normal" response to an "abnormal" and/or dangerous situation. Those who oppose this idea say it is just another way to blame the deceased victim for his own murder.

It is plausible that Susan Wright went into a wild and irrational frenzy during the moment of the crime. However, her husband was tied up, which makes it difficult to imagine that she felt any danger or was afraid of him during that moment—at least it is hard to understand from a rational perspective. Susan was clearly enraged with her husband. After all, it takes a lot of energy to stab someone almost two hundred times, clean up the mess, and then bury the body in the backyard. The question remains, however: Was the murder of Jeffrey Wright revenge or self-defense? Maybe, in Susan Wright's case, it was a little of both.

Unlike Susan Wright, who claimed she had been violently abused, NANCY SEAMAN didn't appear to be a woman with an ax to grind—but she did, driving one into her husband's skull.

Nancy was a gray-haired, fifty-two-year-old teacher who, at a whiff above five feet tall and weighing a scant one hundred pounds, was barely taller than her fourth-grade students.

On May 9, 2004, Nancy bolted from a Mother's Day dinner, following yet another argument with her husband Robert, fifty-seven, and drove to a Home Depot, where she bought a twenty-two-ounce hatchet. Upon her return to their Tudor home in an exclusive subdivision in suburban Detroit, she allegedly walked up behind Robert in the bathroom and struck him in the head with the axlike hatchet. The next day Nancy arrived at school, taught her students, and then made a pit stop on the way home to pick up bleach, rubber gloves, a tarp, and other materials. After cleaning up, she wrapped Robert in the tarp and secured it tightly with duct tape, then placed his body in the back of his Ford Explorer, which was parked in their driveway.

Robert, a local businessman, was reported missing two days later by his brother. Shortly thereafter, police arrived at the Seaman home and questioned Nancy, who claimed her husband had left the house and never returned. When police discovered Robert's body inside his SUV, they found he had more than a dozen axlike wounds to the head, had been stabbed twenty-one times, and his throat was cut. They also found the hatchet, soaked in bleach, under the car seat.

Nancy was arrested and charged with what prosecutors claimed was a methodically planned "cold-blooded murder." They pointed to video taken at the Home Depot that captured her buying an axlike hatchet the night her husband died as well as stealing another one, which she returned two days later using the receipt from the actual purchase, ostensibly to erase the purchase from her credit card.

For her part, Nancy claimed, through her attorney, that she was a woman who had suffered years of abuse at the hands of her husband, who attacked her that Sunday after learning that she secretly put a down payment on a condominium and had been taking items from their home. The couple had been sleeping apart and were planning to divorce, she said, and she was preparing to move on with her life. But her husband's angry reaction startled her, and when he took out a knife and cut her hand, she ran to the garage, where she picked up the hatchet and swung at her husband, killing him.

The killing of Robert Seaman was the end of a marriage that spanned more than thirty years, a marriage that mirrored the lives of any successful family. Robert was the vice president of an engineering firm with a complementary six-figure salary while Nancy was a stay-at-home mom, taking care of their two boys and their $400,000 home in a gated community. But after the children were grown she decided to follow a lifelong dream, and in 1997 she became a teacher in the local public school system.

While many thought the Seamans had a strong relationship, in reality they would often argue loudly. Nancy alleged her husband had been unfaithful, since he spent more time with another woman than he did with his own wife and two sons. She even filed a protection order against the woman, claiming she was trying to destroy her marriage. "It appears she wants my life," said Nancy in her complaint. The stress of her marriage was even causing what Nancy described as "severe loosening of my upper teeth due to grinding." But the core of her defense, she claimed, was the years of abuse she had endured at the hands of her husband, who she said had a vicious temper and habitually kicked and hit her.

Nancy testified that Robert had attacked her nearly a hundred times during their marriage. When he lost his six-figure job in the 1990s, the violence became even more frequent, since Nancy had become the breadwinner and provider of health benefits, a circumstance that she said gnawed at her husband. The beatings became so regular, she said, that she learned to cover her face with her hands or arms. When asked why she never reported any of the beatings to police or filed charges against her husband, Nancy offered vague excuses. When asked why she even stayed in the marriage, Nancy said it was due to her strict Catholic upbringing and, after all was said and done, she still loved Robert dearly.

Her attorney brought in experts to testify about battered women's syndrome, to explain why she remained with her husband all those years, and why there were so many wounds on Robert's body. Nancy, said her attorney, just kept swinging the hatchet to save her own life.

Robert's death divided the family. Son Greg defended his mother, testifying that his father angered easily and was abusive. He also drank heavily, his physical deterioration the result of losing his cushy job several years earlier. But older brother Jeff told a different story, one in which his father was a loving man who was married to a woman prone to injuring herself as a result of clumsiness. Nancy's brother-in-law testified that Robert knew his wife purchased a condo and told her just prior to his death that it would be part of any divorce settlement. That, he testified, was the last straw. Nancy, he said, promptly purchased the hatchet, returned home, and killed her husband.

The jury didn't believe Nancy's testimony, finding it contrived. They also found her to be someone who was easily angered and combative. In the end, they found her guilty of murdering her husband. She was sentenced to life in prison.

LOVE seems to be the unlikely partner of hate, yet when we are strongly connected by love to another person, he or she can stir up a lot of other intense emotions, including stress and displeasure. Both love and hate can become obsessive. Together, these emotions activate the primitive neural system in the brain. Our minds are often occupied by the people who we love and hate because those people often either enhance our reproductive capabilities or threaten our ability to survive. A person who falls "in hate" may spend as much time thinking and brooding about the hated individual as does a person who falls in love. Accompanying hatred, however, is a tremendous amount of aggression and hostility. Hate can blind us and therefore make us think and behave in ways beyond reason. Hate is the most powerful and enduring form of primal hostility.

One thing that separates human beings from other animals is that we often, without knowing it and/or having a valid reason for it, cause each other emotional suffering. We do this by cheating, lying, humiliating, disappointing, betraying, or abandoning one another. And it's fascinating that we often inflict these painful wounds not on our enemies but on the people with whom we feel most close and intimate. It's odd that so much human suffering takes place not on the battlefields of war, but in the private battlefields of our homes, and that it can lead to the destruction of our dreams and hopes for the future. In some cases such intense suffering can lead to an unyielding desire to retaliate and get even. In still other cases it can turn heinously violent. That's what happened in the case of Nancy Seaman and her husband Bob. They were unhappily married for thirty-one years.

Growing up, Nancy Seaman could have been anything she wanted to be. She graduated as valedictorian of her high school class. But all she ever really wanted in life was to be a successful wife and mother. She would often dream of her wedding day and the white picket fence she wanted to live behind. When she met Robert Seaman, she found him to be quite dashing and charming. And when she married him she believed she had met and married the man of her childhood dreams. But the dreams quickly turned into nightmares, leaving young Nancy confused and disenchanted.

The marriage, she said, went sour only two weeks after the ceremony. Nancy was unprepared for Robert's transformation from Dr. Jekyll to Mr. Hyde.

According to Nancy, she continued trying to make their marriage look the way she thought a marriage should look. She tried to be quiet at times, even submissive. She also did her best to be seductive and supportive. In the end, however, it seemed that whatever she did wasn't good enough. The years flew by and the marriage only got worse. Nancy often felt devalued by her husband's continual criticism, and whatever self-esteem she had quickly eroded. She admitted to being temperamentally erratic, yet she always felt that was in response to Robert's provocation. Then there were the affairs, the critiquing of her career aspirations, and his spending less and less time at home. It was as if he despised her. Nancy Seaman's marriage was her own private hell, a hell that often left her isolated and feeling alone. The only person she felt she could rely on was her younger son, Greg.

Robert's dismissive and abusive behavior over the years left Nancy feeling injured and violated, and the marriage was ruining her view of herself and her life. She found her injuries unforgivable and felt that she had no control over her life. Robert had taken everything away from her and she didn't know if she would ever really be able to recover from her intense sense of betrayal. Robert had destroyed her ideas about fairness, justice, predictability, and goodness. It is not uncommon for unforgivable injuries, brought on by a "misbehaving" spouse, to cause a combination of pain, rage, and humiliation. Robert had not only robbed Nancy of her future, but he had destroyed her past and her present as well. From her perspective, her life was a mess and it was all his fault. Robert was supposed to love her and protect her from pain. Instead he just caused her more pain and heartache.

The issues in Bob and Nancy's marriage only grew worse

with time. For example, Nancy began to wonder who would want her now that she was middle aged, and, according to Nancy, Robert delighted in pointing this out to her quite often. Furthermore, she claimed that Robert began to ask her to play the role of a thirteen-year-old schoolgirl before he would have sex with her. This only perpetuated Nancy's theory that the request was linked to the woman he was now spending more of his time with—and that woman had a thirteen-year-old daughter. As time wore on, Nancy felt increasingly defenseless and unable to find her own purpose in life. She felt her husband deserved to be punished for robbing her of her life. It was time that she balanced the scales that had been tipped against her for more than thirty years. In Nancy's eyes, Robert's days were numbered; he just didn't know it yet.

Of course, there are two sides to any story, and it has been argued that Robert wasn't thrilled with his wife's behavior either. According to him, Nancy was unpredictable, irritable, and appeared to have an untreated mood disorder. Yet she refused to get any help and seemed to prefer blaming everybody else for her failures in life. She would scream in front of their friends, accusing him of having affairs that Robert said never happened.

Either way, Nancy Seaman was a woman who had suppressed much rage. Now, it had stewed into a bitter and undeniable resentment, which ultimately turned into a perceived need for revenge. There was no denying the pain and hurt any longer. Nancy had an irrepressible cruel wish to harm her husband in the way he had harmed her over the years. It was an eye-for-an-eye mentality. Her desire to seek revenge was overwhelming. Think *War of the Roses,* only worse.

MOTHER'S Day is supposed to be a special day on which the family celebrates their love and appreciation for the woman/

mother of the house, yet in keeping with the theme of Nancy Seaman's life, Mother's Day was no different from any other. There was no appreciation. She and her husband had agreed to move in different directions. That was all too clear now. There were no flowers, no gifts, just more disappointment and misery.

It's human nature to want to strike out at someone who deeply hurts you. According to a recent study, brain scans reveal that revenge really can, like Dirty Harry says, make your day. Planning revenge can spark enough pleasure to actually motivate getting even. It is the amount of satisfaction that may ultimately predict who will take it to the next level and who will not. People want to punish "wrongdoers." There is a clear connection between emotion and behavior. Our emotions can also influence our analytical decision-making skills. The "revenge study" mentioned above also revealed that the dorsal striatum, the brain region governing enjoyment and satisfaction, became active in the people who decided to retaliate. This activity was not necessarily the exhilaration caused by revenge itself, but rather the pleasure of anticipating it.

When Nancy attacked her husband, the force and nature of the attack represented all of the abuse that she had endured during their thirty-year marriage. With each blow of the hatchet Nancy sighed in relief. Robert could not hurt her anymore.

Marriage is supposed to be a beautiful joint venture. It is a creative and life-enhancing experience; at least it should be. Nancy's had been nothing like that. After it was all done, she carefully wrapped Robert up and placed him in her car. When asked about the wrapped dead body, Nancy said it was artwork. In a way, this was the artistic gift she gave herself after thirty years of marriage. This was all her marriage ever was anyway, a bloody, sad mistake.

10

The Pregnancy Killer

MANY modern magazines and popular TV shows, movies, and commercials depict parenthood as idyllic. The same myths that airbrush the realities of marriage also affect our perceptions of having children. This part of life is often romanticized; having a baby with the person you are in love with would seem to ensure and enhance the relationship. I know I certainly felt this way when I was young. Some women get pregnant because they believe it will help them hold on to their partner, or prevent a problematic relationship from breaking apart. Others believe having a baby can save an ailing marriage. Anyone who has ever had a child knows this belief is far from a sure thing. Parenthood, with all of its wonders, often increases strain and stress on a relationship. Before exploring all of the pathological reasons why pregnancy can be lethal for women, we should first identify some of the normal, yet often masked, parental reactions that can occur. These feelings are rarely discussed, because they are too scary.

Pregnancy can bring up a whole host of strong emotions, not all of them positive. It is normal to fear what is unknown, and having a baby is a big unknown. Both mothers and fathers, no matter how much they think they want a baby, may react to the news of a new pregnancy with overwhelming ambivalence. A pregnancy can bring up deep psychological conflicts. For example, sometimes parents-to-be revisit feelings they once had toward their own parents, and such emotions are often unpleasant. More common reactions toward pregnancy include thoughts such as *I do not want to have this baby; This cannot be true;* and perhaps the most frequent of them all, *My life will be over.* An adult who felt unwanted or unloved by his own parents may find it very hard to want his own unborn child. It is probably safe to say, yet undoubtedly controversial, that no child is wanted 100 percent. Every parent has some degree of mixed feelings about having a child.

But let's revisit one of the thoughts listed above: *My life will be over.* Certainly it is human nature to have such a fear, and yet having children does not really mean the end of one's life. Some of us fear that we must abandon our own pleasures in order to devote ourselves to our children. Truly the birth of our children signifies our replacement by a new generation, and in that sense there is a sort of death in birth. In fact, pregnancy can be experienced as the death of one's youth and childhood, and the death of being responsible exclusively for oneself. However, part of the upside—which is difficult, if not impossible, for some to see—is that the birth of a child can create new opportunities for successful living and feelings of fulfillment.

Another common fear is of giving birth to a monster. As bizarre as this may sound, believe it or not, the "monster" fantasy is almost as ancient as humankind and civilization itself. The drawings on the cavemen's walls, the legends of each primitive society and the ancient Greek myths, all refer to this frightening theme. Roman Polanski's famous film *Rosemary's Baby,* based on Ira Levin's iconic book, is rooted in some of the fears men and women have about pregnancy. First there is this notion that the sex act, which creates the baby, is evil and wicked. And then there is the fear that the woman will give birth to the devil, and that, monster or not, the devil will be loved unconditionally by the mother. Because of this fear, sometimes parents choose to adopt a child simply to avoid any possibility of having a deformed monster child of their own. Again, this highlights how the unknown can be experienced as foreboding and scary.

Still another fear is of the impending financial burdens. Often this rests with the male. Coupled with this fear is the broad notion that one may be unable to handle parenthood psychologically. The parent-to-be fears all of the responsibility involved in bringing up a child. Men, in particular, are very sensitive to the possibility of losing their freedom, and some of them greatly resent it. According to criminal profiler Pat Brown, pregnancy is a huge life-changing event that can be experienced by some men as a major limitation. In certain cases, the birth of a child marks the end of a hedonistic era in which the male has sought pleasure without answering to anyone or being "chained" to a wife and child.

In today's world, however, there is a greater likelihood that the male will be directly involved with the pregnancy. Part of this involvement requires that the male prepare himself psychologically for both pregnancy and parenthood. This task is often harder for men simply because they are further removed from the physical facts of pregnancy and hence, from experiencing their unborn child in the same way that the woman does. Approaching fatherhood can sometimes trigger depression, appetite problems, sleeplessness, a false obsession with having an illness, and in severe cases, even suicide and homicide.

The Scott Peterson trial and Mark Hacking headlines brought national attention to the unpleasant reality that pregnancy can be a dangerous time for some women. The shocking study that pregnancy was the leading cause of murder among pregnant women became widely quoted. In fact, according to a Maryland study published in the *Journal of the American Medical Association*, pregnant women are more likely to die of homicide than any other cause. The high percentage, while utterly confounding, may even be higher than initially reported, as many of these deaths go undetected due to a lack of autopsy reports. While the Maryland study did not explain *why* homicide is the leading cause of death among pregnant women, there are theories that these homicides are in part a result of the societal and historical influences mentioned above. In other words, we live in a patriarchal society wherein some men *still*, whether consciously or not, see women as their property, to be treated any way necessary. Certainly, in Western society, such views are generally discouraged. That being said, simply because something is discouraged does not mean it doesn't exist.

Men who subscribe to this way of thinking tend to be more likely to commit homicide *if* they fall into any of these categories: owning a gun, being with an extremely controlling partner, and/or being unemployed. Additionally, as stated earlier, if the female partner is pregnant against her partner's wishes, the male's aggression factor is ultimately increased. Obviously, not every sexist man who owns a gun, suffers at the hands of a controlling wife, or lacks a job will murder his pregnant wife. Still, there is a chilling trend. As the statistics on this issue become more available, experts are beginning to notice that pregnancy can be an aggravating aspect that increases a woman's risk of being killed.

While maternal homicide has recently received a lot of attention in the mainstream media, considerable research has also been done on battered pregnant women. Some of these studies go back twenty years. According to the American Bar Association, by the most conservative estimate, each year one million women suffer nonfatal violence at the hands of their intimate partner. Yet other sources provide astounding numbers. According to the Women's Rural Advocacy Program, four million women are assaulted and beaten by their partner in a year and 37 percent of pregnant women, across all class, race, and educational lines, have been physically abused during pregnancy.

It is especially hard to imagine an act more horrific than the killing of a pregnant woman. Still worse is the idea that her killer is, most likely, her intimate partner and the father of her unborn child. There are several reasons abusive spouses may focus on harming the fetus, although in most cases there are feelings of neglect on the part of the male spouse. They know any threat to the unborn child will upset the mother-to-be and, understanding the pregnancy is what the woman is most concerned with, will target the fetus and thus return attention to the male.

Additionally, during her pregnancy a woman tends to be overwhelmed by concerned family and friends, and therefore less isolated than she may be ordinarily. This can prove very threatening for an abusive spouse, who may grow jealous over all the attention. Still, other researchers believe abuse from the male can be triggered by the stress brought on via the pregnancy itself, for instance, worries over finances.

Certainly, numerous prompts can become catalysts for abuse, and it would not be surprising for a male to exhibit several of these characteristics, rather than simply one or the other. For example, in many cases, pregnant women are tired, less attentive, and uninterested in sex. Obviously this may contribute to a male's feeling that he has been abandoned. Additionally, some men become paranoid, believing the baby is not theirs but was fathered by another man—yet another indication of neglect and betrayal. And, in still other instances, there are men who see the pregnancy as challenging their idea of manhood, which does not include taking care of babies.

Perhaps the most frightening aspect about this type of murder is that the men who kill their partners, for the most part, rarely exhibit any warning or danger signs. And aside from some of the motivations these killers share, people who kill their pregnant wives often do not fit into any particular forensic profile, crossing all racial barriers and economic classes. Interestingly, one of the only parallels that pregnancy killers exhibit is the murder weapon. Pregnant victims are, more often than not, killed with a gun.

RAE CARRUTH was an upstanding citizen and rising football star. A wide receiver for the Carolina Panthers, he was a polished athlete who enjoyed all that the National Football League had to offer—both on the field, where his job was to catch footballs, and off the field, where he ably caught the attention of some of the most beautiful women in Charlotte, North Carolina. A first-round draft pick out of the University of Colorado in 1997, Carruth received a four-year, $3.7 million contract. His was a success story.

Soon after Carruth's birth in Sacramento, California, his father abandoned the new family. His mother, a social worker, remarried but divorced again when Carruth was in his teens. The family lived in a poverty-stricken, drug-infested neighborhood, but Carruth found sanctuary on the athletic field, excelling at football and becoming a high school star. He was also popular with his fellow students, and this led him to being twice voted to serve as the school's prom king.

Clean cut and handsome at age twenty-six, Carruth juggled multiple girlfriends after arriving in Charlotte, many of them starstruck and impressionable. Among his many admirers was Cherica Adams. A former Panthers intern and topless dancer, Adams, twenty-four, met Carruth at a party in 1999. The two dated, and within a short time Adams became pregnant. Carruth, who already had a son from a previous relationship and paid $3,000 a month in child support, told Adams to abort the pregnancy. She refused, saying she wanted to have the baby.

Her choice angered Carruth. He was in the last year of his contract and had recently made a poor investment decision that had cost him tens of thousands. He was also the subject of a lawsuit in a real estate deal gone sour, and the thought of paying additional child support made him less than enthusiastic about the pregnancy. To further complicate things, he was also romantically interested in another woman, and had no intentions of allowing Adams to remain in his life.

Since Adams understood Carruth had no plans to marry her, she began taking steps toward surviving as a single mother. She took maternity classes and selected her son's name months in advance, excited for the day when her child would be born. As with any pregnancy, without the support of the father, the first few months were difficult. The pair often exchanged angry words, with Adams even confronting Carruth at the stadium following a game, as he was leaving with another woman. Yet Adams did not foresee any danger to her or her unborn child.

On November 15, 1999, with Adams in her seventh month of pregnancy, Rae Carruth decided to take a different tack, and accompanied Adams to the movies. After seeing *The Bone Collector,* a film about a police hunt for a killer, they left in separate cars, with Adams following Carruth to her apartment. A few minutes later a car pulled up alongside Adams and a gunman fired several shots, severely injuring her. Conscious, Adams dialed 911 on her cell phone and told the operator she'd been shot. She also told them who she thought was behind it—Rae Carruth. "I think he did it," she said.

Paramedics soon arrived and took Adams to the hospital, where she was treated for gunshot wounds to the liver, stomach, back, and right lung. They also performed an emergency cesarean section and delivered her boy, who was named Chancellor Lee and born ten weeks early. Adams remained gravely ill for the next month. During that time she provided police with details of the shooting in which she said Carruth, driving ahead in an SUV, stopped in front of her, which forced her to come to a halt in her BMW. At that time, another car pulled up alongside her with several men inside, and shots rang out. Rae Carruth was arrested a week later and charged with conspiracy to commit first-degree murder. The alleged reason? He didn't want to pay child support.

Three other men were eventually arrested, including the triggerman, and all said it was Carruth who hired them to kill his girlfriend. They said he had given them the money to rent the car and to buy a gun. They waited at a nearby gas station for the pair to leave the movie theater, and then followed them along a predetermined route. Cherica Adams died on December 14, and Rae Carruth, who had been free on a $3 million bond, was now wanted for murder. Instead of turning himself in, he fled with a friend to Tennessee, where he was caught several days later hiding in the trunk of a car.

Carruth claimed he was innocent of any crime and didn't even know Adams had been shot until the following morning. But during his subsequent trial the gunman, Van Brett Watkins, a reputed drug dealer with a history of psychological problems, testified to Carruth's involvement in the murder and also said Carruth offered to pay him $5,000 to beat Adams and force a miscarriage. According to Watkins, after some thought, Carruth decided instead to have Adams murdered. Watkins and the other two men all testified that Carruth was at the scene. Additionally, a girlfriend of Carruth testified that he confided to her that he hated Adams for becoming pregnant and forcing him to have a child he did not want.

The jury found Carruth guilty of conspiracy, and he was sentenced to nineteen to twenty-four years in prison. His son, Chancellor, whose life hung in a delicate balance for weeks after his birth, now suffers from multiple sclerosis and lives with his maternal grandmother.

• • •

As a child Rae Carruth was ambitious with a strong focus. He wanted to be a professional football player. In high school he was an all-American boy who was popular with his classmates. At the age of twenty-three he signed his lucrative four-year contract to be a wide receiver for the Panthers. But upon breaking his foot, after only his first season, he became more of a liability than an asset to his team. His expenditures began to exceed his income. In part, pricey child support payments, due to a lost paternity suit, contributed to his spending, and he was now accountable for at least $3,500 a month. This annoyed him tremendously. With money tight and his injury affecting his ability to play football, his future looked somewhat precarious. During this stressful time, Cherica Adams learned she was pregnant with Carruth's child. For Carruth, a ladies' man who enjoyed dating a number of women simultaneously, their relationship had been a casual one. When he asked Adams to get an abortion, her refusal must have disturbed him.

Many professional athletes have a "the world is mine" mentality, and Carruth was certainly no exception. Star athletes command millions of dollars in salary and endorsements and create billions of dollars in revenue for their companies and teams. This places them in such a privileged position that, unfortunately, many acquire a false belief that anything is possible. Some athletes exhibit an exaggerated sense of self-importance, believing that rules don't apply to them. Such stars are also prone to act out their impulsivity aggressively.

Society contributes to this behavior by paying professional athletes more money than they would likely earn any other way. Their life often looks like a fantasy, and to ensure the success of that fantasy, everything revolves around winning. And success fosters a feeling of entitlement. The downside to such thinking is that, inevitably, even star athletes cannot control everything. Cherica Adams was a prime example of something uncontrollable. Carruth was learning this lesson the hard way; first with his lost paternity suit in 1997, and now with this estranged girlfriend's pregnancy. If someone has a narcissistic rage problem (and Rae Carruth fit the profile perfectly) and something uncontrollable goes against the individual, it can trigger homicidal rage. In Carruth's case, his "problem" required him to hire a hit man to do his dirty work for him; the solution meant getting rid of the very pregnant Cherica Adams.

Rae Carruth could not tolerate someone exerting power over him or telling him what to do, particularly when he was feeling insecure about his own professional future. The combination of factors encouraged his murderous impulses. Sadly, many athletes like Carruth do not know what to do without their athletic prowess to count on. It's especially hard for them to adjust to life without the adoration, attention, and hero status once gained through their sport. It would not be surprising if Carruth, with his future career prospects unstable, was feeling vulnerable and in danger. Perhaps the idea of a premature retirement with two children to support was intolerable to him.

Given that Carruth came from a broken home, it was a great feat to rise to the level of football star. Additionally, Carruth's abandonment by his birth father was no doubt etched into his psyche. It is possible that Carruth's interpretation of how his own father felt about him was recycled into Carruth's feelings toward Adams's unborn child. In getting rid of this unborn child and pregnant girlfriend, he becomes like his father (whether he realizes it or not). Many fathers-to-be who, like Carruth, despise their fathers may also fear that their own sons will, in turn, grow up to hate them. Unable to cope with the unknown, Carruth was feeling a loss of freedom that enraged him and, in his case, he would do anything to steal it back.

• • •

CHARLES STEWART also felt entitled. During the early evening hours of October 23, 1989, emergency 911 operators in Boston, Massachusetts, received a frantic call from a desperate man who said he was in his car with his wife and both had been shot. The man, Charles, thirty, was seriously wounded, with a bullet in his stomach. His wife Carol was lying unconscious, with blood pouring from a gaping wound to her head. She was seven months pregnant.

The couple had just attended a childbirth class at a local hospital and were returning to their suburban home, but somehow they had ended up in a crime-ridden, drug-infested neighborhood. During the thirteen minutes that Charles remained on his car phone he begged and pleaded for help while trying to ascertain his condition. Curiously, not once did he try to comfort his wife or even attempt to talk to her. When police arrived, a barely conscious Charles said a mugger had attacked him and Carol. Charles described the mugger as a black man with a raspy voice who took their jewelry and other personal items before opening fire.

Carol died, as did her son Christopher, who was delivered by cesarean section but survived only seventeen days. Charles spent six weeks in the hospital, enduring two operations to repair various organs, and was forced to use a colostomy bag. While recuperating he wrote a farewell letter to his wife that read, in part, "you have brought joy and kindness to every life you've touched. Now you sleep away from me." (The letter later was read by his best friend at Carol's funeral.) Carol's death, as told by her husband, shocked the community and the nation, and fanned racial tensions throughout Boston.

THE Stewarts had been married for four years after meeting at a local restaurant where he was a cook and she was a waitress paying her way through law school. Carol was immediately smitten with Charles, who was outgoing and gregarious. He was the son of a bartender and grew up in a large family in a blue-collar section of Boston. A high school athlete, he had little use for school, and after graduation he lied on a job application, claiming he had attended Brown University on an athletic scholarship. His charming manner got him the job nonetheless, and he eventually earned $100,000 a year managing a Boston fur store. His ultimate goal, though, was to open his own restaurant.

Carol was described as cheery and delightful. She was an attorney who worked for a publishing company. As a couple, the Stewarts appeared perfect, happily entertaining friends on weekends in their suburban home and always telling each other "I love you" at the end of their phone conversations. Yet tensions had developed in their relationship after Carol learned she was pregnant. The news did not sit well with Charles, who believed a baby would derail his plans to open his dream restaurant, and instead keep him ensconced in a job and career he had no desire to continue or pursue. Charles wanted his wife to abort the pregnancy, but she refused.

Just weeks after the shooting, police arrested William Bennett, thirty-nine, an unemployed black man who once shot a police officer, and charged him with Carol's murder. Boston police had stopped and searched nearly every black man in the neighborhood, infuriating civil rights leaders along with residents, but they believed they had their man in Bennett, who was said to have told a nephew that he had been involved in Carol's murder. Charles had picked Bennett out from a police lineup. The mayor of Boston was present for the announcement of Bennett's arrest.

With the chief suspect now in custody, Charles moved forward with his life, cashing in Carol's life insurance, which included an $82,000 check and, over time, additional payments totaling over $100,000. But just after New Year's, in 1990, Charles's brother, Matthew, made a startling admission: He knew his brother Charles had killed Carol Stewart.

Following William Bennett's arrest, a guilt-ridden Matthew confessed to a dozen friends and relatives that his brother was the real culprit. For weeks the brothers had grappled over their secret, unsure of what to do. But in early January, Matthew told his story to police. In his shocking account, Matthew admitted conspiring with Charles to stage a fake robbery of Carol's jewelry, ostensibly to cash in on the jewelry insurance money.

The brothers had staged a practice run the night before, said Matthew, and on the night of the murder Matthew pulled up alongside his brother's car, but was unaware that Carol had been shot. Charles, said Matthew, reached out and handed him a bag filled with jewelry, his watch, and a gun. When Charles learned that his brother had confessed to the police, he drove to a bridge during the early morning hours and jumped into the icy water below. His body was found the next day.

During grand jury testimony just a few weeks later, a friend testified that Charles had asked him to help him get rid of Carol. Her pregnancy was a roadblock to his plans to open a restaurant. Charles, said the friend, wanted to work for himself, not others.

Additionally, his relationship with a former coworker was revealed. She was twenty-three, and police learned she had used Charles's credit cards to call him in the hospital. Police also learned that Charles had bought her a gold brooch two days before he killed himself.

CHARLES enjoyed the sympathy and support of the media when he informed the Boston police a black mugger injured him and killed his pregnant wife. No one ever suspected this handsome, successful businessman would ever be involved in such a heinous and brutal crime. Yet, although the Stewarts appeared to be a happy and devoted couple on the outside, Charles always seemed to have another agenda that was very difficult for people to access. If one could unlock his mysterious side, they would have gained a glimpse into his dark and more sinister motivations. Underneath the good looks and well-paying job was a man with antisocial personality disorder. The nature of the disorder is that of rage.

Charles's rage was carefully masked, but nevertheless very present. Like many people with personality disorder tendencies, Charles was manipulative. He appeared to be charming, but his charm masked his self-serving nature. He expected unconditional surrender from the people around him and believed that he was entitled to everything he wished for. Some theorists believe that people who are diagnosed with antisocial personality disorder are, like everyone else, people with a deep wish to be loved and cared for. Despite the outside overconfidence, Charles felt inferior to others.

Charles had a tendency to feel bored and empty. Life never fully offered him the excitement and feelings of importance he craved. When he first met and married Carol, he thought that her lifestyle and her impressive career as a lawyer would give him status in the world that had previously escaped him. In the 1980s, it was all about "yuppie" status. He had achieved that, but it still was not enough for him. He needed more.

Charles needed excessive stimulation in order to feel fully alive; it was his way of warding off a debilitating and paralyzing depression. As we now know, Charles had a very violent self-destructive side that he fought to assuage, and as much as he had a tendency to target his aggression toward others, he also had a tendency to target it toward himself. The effect of such internal aggression was severe. Charles began to wonder if life was really meaningless. The only thing that kept him going was his dream to become a famous and successful restaurateur and yet, as we also know, he believed that Carol's pregnancy would put an end to that dream.

Prior to resorting to murder, and to escape the realities of parenthood, Charles began to go out more with the guys, which greatly upset his very pregnant wife. On some level she knew that he was avoiding her. She also felt emotionally abandoned. Moreover, unbeknownst to his wife, Charles had a deepening attachment to a younger, single, unpregnant woman.

According to Joseph Scalia, author of *Intimate Violence*, some men have a Madonna/whore mentality when it comes to their wife's pregnancy. It is one thing for a wife to have sex; it is quite another thing for her to enjoy it. To some of these men, a wife's enjoyment of her pregnancy makes her seem vulgar. It may be one thing to have sexual relations, but it is quite another thing to advertise that one has sex and even likes it. For such men, pregnancy means just that, that a woman not only has sex, but likes it—which makes women seem like whores.

Men with Charles's personality problems can either be fascinated or terrified by the thought of having children: Charles was terrified. A child can be unconditionally adoring or completely demanding, diverting important attention away from oneself. A baby consumes a lot of time, energy, resources, emotions, and attention. Charles knew in his heart that a baby would be a menace to his life and that it was utterly unnecessary for him to have one.

According to Dr. Hyman Spotnitz, a founder of modern psychoanalysis, the desire to abort a child can reflect an unconscious desire to kill off one's siblings—especially if hatred toward a sibling is particularly intense. Interestingly, Charles Stewart came from a family with many siblings. Theories suggest that an individual's reason for not wanting a baby of his own can sometimes stem from wishing that his mother had eliminated the baby that later became his younger sibling. Furthermore, fatherhood itself can also bring up unhappy memories of rivalry with brothers and sisters.

It is interesting that Charles decided to enlist his brother

Matthew for help. Charles and Matthew got along very well, and some believe that Matthew experienced their childhood in the same way, imagining that there was never enough room for everyone. Additionally, neither wanted to end up like their father, who was a man always struggling and giving to everyone else rather than himself.

Charles carried through with his murderous and devious plan. He suffered some pretty painful wounds himself. While only intending to shoot his foot, he managed to shoot his abdomen instead. He needed multiple surgeries and ultimately had to have a colostomy bag. Is it possible he felt some degree of guilt about killing his pregnant wife? He left himself with horrible wounds; he ultimately confessed to the murder before finally killing himself. Perhaps his suicide had more to do with not wanting to face the shame of being a convicted killer than with really caring about killing his pregnant spouse. Perhaps the prospect of being exposed was just too much for him to handle. Or maybe Charles Stewart had a suicidal personality all along, that up until this point he had successfully defended against. All of the materialism and striving to be more was an attempt to deal with his feelings of inadequacy for who he really felt he was, a dumb nobody who came from nothing and still was nothing.

Certain spousal killers may have a powerful suicidal drive that they try to obstruct by killing others. These killers often feel that others are preventing them from living their lives as they wish to. But these feelings may actually be about themselves. They may believe on some level that they should not be alive and/or should really be dead. Instead of making a suicidal presentation, they present the opposite—that of entitlement. Ultimately, however, they are fighting against this powerful suicidal impulse. When killing another does not work for them, they end up doing what they really wanted to do all along—kill themselves.

11

The Caregiver Killer

ALTHOUGH some people find caring for a sick or gravely ill spouse to be a satisfying experience, for many it can have a profoundly negative consequence filled with anxiety and depression. Caregivers often feel overburdened, overwhelmed, and constantly in demand. And when they believe the person they're taking care of is unreasonable, unappreciative, and manipulative, they also complain of higher levels of stress.

Spousal caregivers are at a great risk to abuse and become violent. It's not the stress that causes the violence, but the mood disturbances that follow the care. Caretakers who lack sufficient income experience this situation as beyond their control. They often lack the problem-solving skills or social support that these circumstances demand, thus triggering a sequence of events that can create a lethal outcome, including murder/suicide.

Before this phenomenon was studied more extensively, the murder of a terminally ill spouse was considered to be a mercy killing, compassionate homicide, or a killing of mutual consent. But in recent years such thinking has become negotiable. Many think that mutual-consent killing is not an act of love or adoration at all, but a sign of desperation and depression. Indeed, the caregiver murder is not an impulsive act, but is planned and prompted by a decline in physical health, or a pending move to an assisted-living facility or nursing home.

Interestingly, the perpetrator tends to be a few years older than his or her spouse and the sick spouse often talks about wanting to die, or professes that he or she would be better off dead. Such isolation and desperation, on the part of the caregiver, eventually becomes too much to bear.

For Roswell Gilbert, there was no other choice.

Roswell, seventy-six, was a retired electronics engineer who had been married for fifty-one years to his beloved wife, Emily. They lived in a seaside condominium off the Florida coast, and prior to becoming ill, Emily had been extremely self-sufficient, independently visiting the beauty salon every two weeks. But that was a long time ago. It was now eight years later and Emily, seventy-three, suffered from a variety of illnesses, including arthritis, Alzheimer's disease, and osteoporosis (all emotionally debilitating and physically painful). As the pain worsened, Emily begged her husband to kill her, to help end her suffering. "I'm so sick," she would say. "I want to die."

On March 4, 1985, Roswell pointed a gun to his wife's head and fired twice, killing her. Roswell described it as an "act of love." Authorities saw it as murder and he was arrested, tried, and found guilty. He was sentenced to serve twenty-five years in prison. But five years after his conviction, frail and sickly, he was granted clemency.

• • •

During the twilight years, marriage has a unique set of challenges. The joyful advertisements that portray retired/older couples walking along a scenic beach together, holding hands, playing golf, bicycling, or vacationing together are beautiful pictorial images. Yet they are often little more than beautiful images. When you look at these pleasant ads, you are meant to assume that the dreams of these loving couples are jointly being met by one another. Such a notion is a wonderful romantic epiphany—let us hope we all have such a time in life to be blissful, and to at last enjoy the comforts of intimacy and togetherness.

But like many idealistic images, there can be danger in such assumptions. There is no guarantee that two people, during their final phase of marriage, will share the same vision for what they want for themselves or their lives. Marital renegotiation during this phase is often urgent and intense. There can be the sense that this is the last chance for a couple to fulfill their personal dreams and destiny.

There is also the pain of loss during this time of life—not only the loss of social connections and work, but an even greater one: friends and relatives. Imagine for a moment that you are in your mid-seventies. Now imagine all of your friends and loved ones. How many of them are still alive at seventy-five? How many are about to die? And if, like you, they are *generally* healthy, how healthy is that? In other words, the life of a senior citizen is often fraught with depression over loss, and not simply loss of one's wellness and mobility but also the colossal loss of time. All of us know the magnitude of time, but who better to understand it than those experiencing its last hours. Beneath the immediate demands of the caregiver is a layer of grief for all that has passed or is passing, and for the individuals and places that are vanishing.

Moreover, due to lack of mobility, and often, the dire state of the sickly, elderly couples are much less involved with the outside world. This makes them far more mutually dependent. As we know, socially isolated individuals are much more prone to manage their frustration and stress in aggressive, self-destructive, and sometimes abusive ways and are more prone to depart from their earlier "appropriate" codes of behavior. They can develop patterns of behavior that otherwise would have remained foreign to them had they had closer relationships, and thus were observed or watched by others. And while witnesses or outside support systems can help dysfunctional couples keep it together much more than they would if left to their own devices, there is a tendency among such couples not to permit intervention.

The most common reason that the elderly fail to seek outside help is separation anxiety. For example, should neighbors or social workers visit the home, there is always a threat that someone might insist the unwell partner be moved to a hospital or nursing facility. Rarely do couples welcome such a change, and in most cases, such a move is avoided at all costs. Additionally, there is a tendency for denial on the part of the caregiver. *The New York Times* featured an editorial on August 21, 2005, entitled, "Will We Ever Arrive at the Good Death?" The story examined the pros and cons of palliative care, and stated that in most cases, patients do not enter into hospice care until two weeks prior to their death. This illustrates how resistant we can be, not only to the reality of death but to the influences of unfamiliar help.

The denial and refusal of aid deprives a couple of much-needed time apart, which may include pursuing separate interests outside of the marriage. A lack of separateness and interpersonal space can cause couples to grow bored with each other and to experience their routines as tedious. For individuals stuck in this rut, there is nothing new to report to one another, no new and exciting experiences to share, which can lead a couple to feel that there is nothing to talk about. They begin to stop feeling curious about each other and, in turn, the relationship becomes one of mere dependency. When you add the pressure of illness to this picture, the situation can be quite disastrous.

As discussed, incessant togetherness is often required of the partner who is taking on the role of caretaker, and therefore, a healthy interpersonal distance may no longer be a realistic option. Private irritations can take over and replace loving feelings that once existed. The illnesses of old age can feel like a curse not only for the spouse who is sick, but for the spouse who is not. The caretaking responsibilities become the responsibility of the "healthy" spouse whose wellness is often only relative. Sometimes the decrease in marital satisfaction is due more to the loss of companionship than to the illness itself. Couples can become depressed and overwhelmed by strong and persistent feelings of hopelessness and helplessness. These feelings, combined with social isolation, can lead to desperation, and, in the worst-case scenario, to murder.

Some of the circumstances that contribute to abuse by a caregiver include a lack of caregiving skills, and in some instances the abuse is a continuation of abuse that went on in the marital relationship before the spouse got sick. Intergenerational and marital violence can continue into old age. If a woman has not reported the abuse that occurred during her fifty-year marriage, she is not likely to report this abuse when she is old, sick, and even more vulnerable due to poor health. In some cases, she may not even label the behavior as abusive, especially if the abuse started when the relationship began.

In many cases such abused women "successfully" made a life for themselves with family, friends, possessions, and traditions. This "success" contributes to their loyalty toward their spouse and their denial about the potential danger they may be in. Sometimes a woman who has been abused for many years may turn the tables on her husband and direct all of her pent-up rage toward him when his health fails and he has become incapable of defending himself. Interestingly, as we have learned, while most domestic violence victims are women, there are more female abusers among older couples than younger couples.

Additionally, very often the caregiver/spouse's personal problems lead the abusive behavior to turn violent and/or lethal. A combination of caregiver stress, emotional or mental illness, addiction to substances, financial stress, and dependency and other personal problems and frustrations can force the caregiver to behave violently in order to "solve" his or her problems. In some instances it's the cared-for spouse who becomes physically abusive. This is more likely to happen when an older spouse suffers from Alzheimer's or other forms of dementia. Caregiver stress is a significant risk factor in neglect and abuse. When a caregiver, especially an elderly sickly one, is pushed into the demands of daily intensive care without any training or information on how to balance his or her needs with the needs of an elderly spouse, it can lead to intense frustration and anger that can too easily turn violent.

Some studies reveal that caregiver stress is often not the primary cause of spousal abuse. Instead the abuse may stem from issues of control and power. The risk of this type of abuse is greater when the caregiver is solely responsible for an elderly spouse who is sick and/or is physically or mentally impaired. Spouses turned caregivers, under these stressful conditions, can often feel trapped, hopeless, resentful, and they may be unaware of available resources and assistance. The caregiver with impaired problem-solving skills or an emotional or personality disorder may not be able to control his or her impulses when feeling enraged or agitated toward his or her spouse.

So, how does this happen and how does it go undetected? Some think certain societal issues are to blame. Ageism and our negative mind-set about older individuals can lead to cultural blindness about the dangers of these caregivers turned murderers. Even worse, a lack of respect for the elderly can contribute to violence against them. Too often older persons remind us of our own mortality, which frightens us. We tend to look away from what scares us. As one result, the older population is sometimes seen as disposable. This view may lead the community to fail to ensure that this vulnerable population lives a nonabusive, supportive, and dignified life. The belief in the value of privacy and the notion that what happens in the home stays in the home can also contribute to older married couples being locked into abusive situations.

ROSWELL Gilbert may be the perfect example of a caregiver killer, whose hopelessness, social isolation, and depression got the better of him and his wife of fifty years. He claimed killing his wife was an *act of love* and that Emily Gilbert not only wanted him to do it, but instructed him to do it. Like many elderly couples who are dealing with extreme stress, the Gilberts found themselves alone and closed in with no one to consult with but each other. Outside support and help was not incorporated into their mind-set and was therefore not looked for.

Roswell and Emily were jointly feeling depressed and hopeless about their lives and about their future. In addition to feeling sorry for his wife, Roswell no doubt felt overburdened and scared. Taking control of ending a sick person's life, who's going to die anyway, can seem to offer relief. That's why he was so easily convinced. He also loved the Emily who was well and did not know how to deal with the Emily who was sick. His confusion led him to take matters into his own lethal hands.

While one might conclude that the above case is much more about mercy killing than abuse, again, there remains the argument that outside intervention could have allowed Emily Gilbert to die a more dignified death. Additionally, due to a lack of intervention it is hard to know what shape Roswell and Emily's relationship was in at the time of the murder. For example, was Emily of sound mind when she asked her husband to kill her? Furthermore, taking into account the strain caring for the elderly can cause, was Roswell of sound mind when he performed the killing?

In this regard, the conclusion that a mercy killing has taken place is not so easy to make. And while the subject is certainly controversial, the Gilbert case is not as clear cut as the ones previously discussed in this book—still, the fact remains that Emily's death *was* murder. Moreover, due to isolated circumstances leading up to that death, one must take into consideration that such a killing was not unlike other spousal murders. In the end, Roswell Gilbert had the ability to control whether or not his wife lived another day. He chose to pull the trigger.

12

Thou Shalt Not Kill

WHO is more dangerous, the wife or the husband?

There's a long-held belief that violence is primarily a male trait; it is a belief that underscores the enduring idea that women create and men destroy. According to researchers Flanagan and Maguire, men commit about 85 percent of all murders and non-negligent manslaughters in the United States.

Why are men more violent? The ongoing argument that the hormone testosterone is a major culprit in male aggression is certainly valid; after all, men produce about twenty-five times more testosterone than females. Still, testosterone alone does not lead a person to commit violence. So, what is the answer?

A starting point would be societal. Let's face it: Our culture (consciously or unconsciously) still encourages men to be strong and handle their disputes in a "manly," "macho," and often physical way. This kind of socialization, combined with other factors—such as psychological disorders or childhood trauma, to name only two—can, under the "right" conditions, convert aggression into violence and homicide.

After finishing her 2001 study *Women Who Kill*, researcher Debbie Kirkwood said, "The reason men commit the vast majority of violent crime in our society is not because they are biologically predisposed to it but because we believe that they are." According to the U.S. Department of Justice, between 1976 and 2002, nearly 11 percent of all murders were committed by an intimate partner. And, of all female murder victims, the percentage of those killed by an intimate remained stable until 1995, when it began to increase. Today nearly a third of all female murder victims are killed by a spouse or lover.

"Everyone starts out totally dependent on a woman. The idea that she could turn out to be your enemy is terribly frightening."

—Lord Astor, British philanthropist, 1993

Women are fully capable of killing, and when it comes to an intimate partner, they kill in chillingly higher numbers. As explained earlier in the book, in spousal/partner murders, women kill seven men for every ten women killed by a man. While the killing itself is nearly the same, a double standard is applied to our view of male violence vs. female violence. We tend to see female violence as abnormal and male violence as normal.

Even today, cultural influences still define women as innately passive and, at their worst, irrational or unstable. Women, being the weaker and more vulnerable sex, are therefore more likely to be viewed as mentally unstable rather than capable of premeditated murder. And many of us still see women as gently maternal, making it impossible to perceive the female as lethal and dangerous.

Interestingly, some women will use the innocent feminine image and/or "I'm just really too small" defense—because it works. Culturally, we're not trained to view young, pretty, polite, and seemingly decent women as dangerous or as possible criminals. Their aggression tends to get trivialized and sexualized and we're shocked when they are accused of violent crimes. Women still receive preferential treatment in the criminal justice system, and women tend to receive lighter jail sentences compared to those for men who commit similar crimes.

Culture also has an impact on the way men and women explain their crimes. Since women are viewed as less dangerous than men, the language used to explain their aggression is much more forgiving and limited. On the other hand, men can't rely on this strategy. For example, you won't hear a man say, "You know, I did murder that woman, but it was because I was having a very bad testosterone-level day." This statement conflicts with our ideas about men, that they are strong, aggressive, and macho.

In terms of spousal murders, men and women kill for very different reasons. Men tend to kill over sexual struggles and choices, while women tend to point to abuse as the precipitating cause for killing a spouse. An equal number of women and men admit to killing their partner for financial gain. More men than women will kill over an argument about money, or because they have been nagged incessantly. Men tend to kill their wives using more aggressive means, like handguns and knives, but of course, there are exceptions. Women, too, will use guns, but they more often utilize blunt instruments, poison, or hired hit men (again there are exceptions).

Men who commit uxoricide—the killing of a wife—often tell their wives what they are going to do prior to committing the crime. What's unnerving about this is that men who kill their female partner or spouse do not exhibit standard risk factors associated with traditional killers.

For example, the traditional male killer or male-on-male killer is more likely to come from a dysfunctional background. Often this killer comes from a broken family or had a father who abused drugs, had a criminal record, or was violent toward his mother. Additionally, in many cases, the killer has had three or more primary caretakers in childhood and has, for varying reasons, been admitted to an institution prior to age sixteen. The intimate-partner killer, however, has more often had a reasonably normal background. Although many had some problems during childhood, overall, this killer has had a fairly traditional family and childhood. It is also of note that a high percentage of male spousal killers tend to have more education and are more likely to be gainfully employed. In effect, the male spousal killer is harder to detect.

Still, there are some signs. One common characteristic of the intimate-partner killer is that he appears to specialize in showing and exhibiting violence toward women. Additionally, this killer is more likely to have a history of problematic relationships with females, including a string of broken relationships. Of note, the intimate-partner killer has also proved, in many instances, to be sober when murdering the victim. Most intimate-partner homicides have involved some kind of ongoing dispute associated with the relationship. And yet, here we must ask ourselves, what relationship doesn't have disputes?

Women who kill their husbands, on the whole, have the least extensive criminal records. This is why some believe they often receive lesser sentences for their crimes when they are convicted. Typical motives for women who kill are jealousy, rage, response to battering, self-defense, and financial gain. Often, as does her male parallel, female killers suffer from psychological problems. Again, as with men, some of these women have been exposed to extreme problems in their parents' marriage during their own childhood and have thereby learned to use violence to solve problems.

Many women who have suffered childhood abuse lack an important foundation of security that helps them to function, feel emotion, and therefore participate completely in the world, leaving these women with a greater chance of becoming killers. Being abandoned and not wanted or cared for can cause any child to feel deep shame, anger, and depression, which can then be expressed in rage, violence, and ultimately murder.

So now that we know the general traits of a killer, what would it take to push you or someone you know to take another person's life? Most people, when asked this question, admit a willingness to kill someone under the *right* circumstances; for example, to save themselves or to protect their child.

The reality is, we all have psychological circuits that direct our brain to contemplate murder, which is why so many of us have thoughts about killing someone at one time or another. After all, that's why "Thou shalt not kill" is one of the Ten Commandments. We're instructed not to do it because we're inclined to do it. For the average person, killing is merely a fantasy, an urge most of us would never act upon, yet such fantasies are very common. That's because our minds are giving us the opportunity to weigh the risks, to consider the cost of such dire action, while at the same time providing us with a cathartic release—and all without our having to act in a destructive way.

Still, we think about murder, and often. Murder fascinates us, in part because the desire to kill another comes from the deepest part of us, our unconscious. The aggressive impulse to eliminate is nature's way of helping us to survive, to protect us from danger, from those who threaten our lives. The disturbing truth is that the only difference between the person who commits murder and the person who does not is that one has decided to act upon the homicidal fantasy.

There are multiple reasons why a person might kill: hate, jealousy, envy, spite, fear, greed, and revenge. All of these emotions—deep-seated thought patterns, internal dialogues, and justifications—predispose us all to consider the lethally unthinkable. Some of the frequent questions I have been asked on television are, *Can anyone become murderous? What is the difference between couples who just get angry with each other and those who actually kill? Why not divorce? Are people born killers? Is there any way to know if you are in danger of marrying someone capable of killing you?*

The scary thing is that anyone can become a victim of marital homicide because anyone can become violent. Dr. Phyllis Sharp, associate professor of nursing at Johns Hopkins, believes marital homicide is less about anger and more about control and an imbalance of power. Sometimes the abuse in a relationship is more subtle, like a partner being unfaithful or a spouse knowing how to make his partner feel bad about herself, and hence powerless.

When people are in a relationship that is equal, both have the skills to deal with their conflicts in a sophisticated, less impulsive way. Forensic expert and regular TV pundit Dr. Michael Welner states that solving conflicts depends on how the anger is expressed. And for most people, verbal communication is enough to help arrive at a nonviolent resolution of conflict.

Joseph Scalia, psychoanalyst and author of the book *Intimate Violence,* offers a provocative idea—that there is little difference between the spouse who cheats and the person who kills, as opposed to the person who won't cheat at all. The person who doesn't cheat has some understanding of the realities of relationships and has come to terms with his inner demons. He accepts the difficulties of life without needing to always meet his needs and have his way and is in relatively little danger of acting impulsively. People who cheat want their needs met. They have a more egocentric approach to the world, and sometimes murder can seem like the fastest way to meeting their needs. Divorce is usually not an option. The spouse can be resistant, there's usually a financial loss, or timing is a factor; yet in many cases, divorce does not satisfy the need to exact revenge or enforce one's self-image. In some cases, the killer wishes to be seen as a widow or widower. In other cases murder is chosen over divorce simply because the spouse believes it is the easier option and that he or she can get away with it.

According to psychoanalyst Dr. Patricia Bratt, you may not be able to sense the less obvious signs of a killer spouse until you are with a person for a long time. Let's face it, we don't really know our partner in depth until we are married to him or her or have lived together for many, many years. I am reminded of a quote I once saw stitched on a pillowcase: "Love is blind and marriage is an eye opener." Marriage can bring up new issues in a way that dating or short-term relationships cannot. We do not always know someone's odd peculiarities until a strange or dramatic event happens. This possibility always exists within a marriage or long-term relationship. When we are dating someone, we often put our best selves forward and do not reveal the darker side of our personalities.

Of particular interest is that many of the spousal killers addressed throughout this book were loved by their in-laws prior to the crime. How can this be? Well, as we have learned, spousal killers can be quite lovable. The nonhomicidal aspect of their personalities can be charming and very pleasant. They can successfully split off the unlovable, dangerous parts when they are not feeling enraged or entitled. In the more psychopathic cases, the homicidal spousal killer deliberately manipulates people in order to be seductive, lovable, and to get his or her own way. Perhaps even more striking is that a spouse can love his or her partner and kill them at the same time. In some cases such individuals do not necessarily want to kill their partner, they just want to get rid of the unlovable part of their spouse and keep the rest.

OF course, murder doesn't just happen out of nowhere. People don't just snap without any warning signs. There are *always* signs, but sometimes these signs are easier to detect in retrospect. Sometimes the signs are subtle. According to Joseph Scalia, unless you are sensitive enough to perceive these subtle symbols, it is possible to miss them altogether. Although there is no perfect way for professionals to predict who will become violent, there are certain markers to keep in mind: high frequency of violence, depression, controlling psychological treatment; and in male killers, poor ideas about women, dependency, physical violence in childhood, possession of weapons, use of drugs or alcohol, and threats to kill and/or to commit suicide. Of course, having these traits does not by any means define you or your spouse as a killer. No, these traits are merely symptoms exhibited by many spousal killers.

One of my hopes in writing this book is to raise awareness and shine a light on an issue that is often misunderstood. In a culture that romanticizes romance and violence, lethal combinations can result under the "right" circumstances. We all want our love lives to be perfect and to meet all of our needs for intimacy. This strong desire or wish often doesn't prepare us for the realities of life and love. Life is challenging and so is love. As long as there is a failure to acknowledge and accept what it means to be truly human we will always be at the mercy of our impulsive nature. When we idealize happiness and what it means to be happy, the frustrations of life can make any of us vulnerable to anger, and eventually to violence.

As individuals, we need to be aware that romantic fantasies are just that. Marriage is not going to solve our problems or make them go away. Marriage does not change anyone. If someone is dangerous or problematic these characteristics often get worse with intimacy, not better. If we have self-destructive tendencies we need to remedy them before choosing our partners.

On a societal level, we need to be very careful about the messages we send out about violence, power, and the "right" way to solve problems. We are all connected. If the neighbors down the street have serious problems, this can have a ripple effect. We need to expand our view of community and get involved, make sure that we invest and make it our business when families are struggling, and we need to support resources that study and encourage the minimization of violence both in and outside the home.

While intimate-partner violence remains part of our culture, there is one good note: The actual number of homicides has declined. In part, this is due to our increased awareness of domestic violence and the increasing support resources that help struggling spouses. While one murder is one too many, this is a problem we all have the power to change. With that sentiment, I do hope this book has provided you with the right awareness, and that these stories will continue to educate and promote the understanding of threatened spousal relationships.

Acknowledgments

DR. ROBI LUDWIG:

I have always believed that our lives are only as good as the people we place in them, and I have been blessed with some amazing people who have entered into my life. Without them, I would not be who I am today; to each I owe enormous gratitude.

First I would like to thank my literary agent, Andrew Stuart, for finding me, choosing me as a client, and suggesting I write this book. This work was his idea and without him *Till Death Do Us Part* would not exist. I also want thank my wonderful cowriter, Matt Birkbeck. Matt not only served as my cowriter, but he also became my supportive teacher and encouraging friend; I have enormous respect for his talent and skills. I also want to thank my television agent, Julie Eckhert, who has been with me from the very start. Thank you for seeing the possibility in me and my career and for having the vision to see how a psychotherapist would fit in the conservative world of TV news. As I have told you many times, Julie, I am so happy I found you! And to David Schifter, my first TV boss, who is now a good friend: You gave me my initial TV exposure and helped me to find my voice as a writer.

This acknowledgment would not be complete if I didn't take a chance to thank the other very special people I've been blessed enough to work with in the television business: Thank you, Ms. Nancy Grace! You have been both a wonderful friend and inspiration to me. Not only do I love working with you but you always remind me to never forget the true purpose of why we do what we do on the air. Thank you, Larry King, for making me feel like a part of your *Larry King Live* family. Appearing on *Larry King Live* has been a real gift, a genuine pleasure, and a major highlight in my professional career. Thank you to Wendy Walker, executive producer of *Larry King Live,* Dean Sicoli, former senior producer of *Larry King Live* and current executive producer of *Nancy Grace,* and Hunter Waters, producer of *Larry King Live,* for inviting me to talk to a worldwide audience about such interesting and stimulating cases as the Scott Peterson trial and the Mark Hacking case. Thank you also to my friends at Court TV, who are a pleasure to work with and forever helpful; the pictures you afforded me for this book illuminated the research being discussed. Michelle Richmond, Ysaacc Sanchez, Diana Palmetiero, and Alicia Cascardi, I give you an enormous thanks. Thank you to Atria for choosing to publish my book and to Wendy Walker, my gifted editor, who worked her inimitable magic on this manuscript. You're the best!

On a personal note, I want to thank two very important mentors in my life, Dr. Vicki Semel and Dr. Patricia Bratt, who have not only guided me personally but professionally and helped me to become the therapist I am today. Thank you to my family for your patience and understanding during all of the time it took to complete this enormous project. I know it was not always easy on you. And of course, thank you to my friends for your curiosity about my book and for supporting and taking pleasure in my professional achievements and success. I really appreciate you being in my life. You all mean the world to me!!!!!!

And finally, a very big Thank You to my husband, David, who is forever a positive force and an inspiration in my life.

MATT BIRKBECK:

When the phone call came from my literary agent, Andrew Stuart, asking if I'd be interested in cowriting a book about marriage and murder, I was somewhat resistant. I knew about the murder part, having covered far too many violent and tragic stories for a host of publications. And I knew about the marriage part, having been joined at the hip to my beautiful wife Donna for fourteen years. But I never really considered the deep-rooted reasons why a spouse would harm his or her significant other, much less take a life.

Needless to say I had a lot to learn, and after an initial meeting with Dr. Robi Ludwig at a Manhattan coffee shop in the dead of winter, I was hooked.

So thanks go to Andrew for bringing this idea to life, to Wendy Walker at Atria Books for her enthusiastic support and editing prowess, and of course, many thanks to Robi, whose commitment, boundless energy, exceptional work ethic, and deep insight made this a fascinating and very worthwhile project.

Intimate-Partner Violence: Links

American Institute on Domestic Violence
2116 Rover Drive
Lake Havasu City, AZ 86403
Phone: 928-453-9015
www.aidv-usa.com

The American Institute on Domestic Violence offers on-site workshops and conference presentations addressing the corporate cost of domestic violence in the workplace.

Asian and Pacific Islander Institute on Domestic Violence
942 Market Street, 2nd Floor
San Francisco, CA 94102
Phone: 415-954-9964
www.apiahf.org/apidvinstitute

The Asian and Pacific Islander Institute on Domestic Violence is a national network that works to raise awareness in Asian and Pacific Islander communities about domestic violence; expand leadership and expertise within Asian and Pacific Islander communities about prevention, intervention, advocacy, and research; and promote culturally relevant programming, research, and advocacy by identifying promising practices.

California Coalition Against Sexual Assault (CALCASA)

1215 K Street, Suite 1100
Sacramento, CA 95814
Phone: 916-446-2520
www.calcasa.org/index.html

CALCASA hosts moderated discussion forums that focus on public health approaches to preventing violence against women. These publicly accessible, multidisciplinary discussion forums are moderated by experts in public health, domestic violence, and sexual assault and are designed to build a broad community of practice for ending all forms of violence against women.

Center for Substance Abuse Prevention

http://pathwayscourses.samhsa.gov/

The Center for Substance Abuse Prevention offers free Web-based courses. Courses deal with identifying problems and risk factors, screening and assessment tools, prevention and intervention strategies, tools for clients, and legal issues surrounding IPV. Various courses offer continuing education credits and are designed for professionals as well as the general public.

Communities Against Violence Network

www.cavnet2.org

Communities Against Violence Network (CAVNET) provides an interactive, online database of information; an international network of professionals; and real-time voice conferencing with professionals and survivors from all over the world, via the Internet. CAVNET seeks to address violence against women, youth violence, and crimes against people with disabilities.

CORPORATE ALLIANCE TO END PARTNER VIOLENCE

2416 E Washington Street, Suite E
Bloomington, IL 61704-4472
Phone: 309-664-0667
www.caepv.org

The Corporate Alliance to End Partner Violence (CAEPV) is a national, nonprofit alliance of corporations and businesses throughout the United States and Canada, working to aid in the prevention of partner violence. CAEPV provides technical assistance and materials to help corporations and businesses address domestic violence in the workplace.

FAITHTRUST INSTITUTE

2400 45th Street, Suite 10
Seattle, WA 98103
Phone: 206-634-1903
www.faithtrustinstitute.org

Formally known as the Center for the Prevention of Domestic and Sexual Violence, FaithTrust Institute is an interreligious educational resource addressing issues of sexual and domestic violence. Its goal is to engage religious leaders in the task of ending abuse and to prepare human-services professionals to recognize and attend to the religious questions and issues that may arise in their work with women and children in crisis.

FAMILY VIOLENCE PREVENTION FUND

383 Rhode Island Street, Suite 304
San Francisco, CA 94103-5133
Phone: 415-252-8900
www.endabuse.org

For more than two decades, the Family Violence Prevention Fund (FVPF) has worked to end violence against women and children around the world. Instrumental in developing the landmark Violence Against Women Act passed by Congress in 1994, FVPF has continued to break new ground by reaching new audiences, including men and youth; promoting leadership within communities to ensure that violence prevention efforts become self-sustaining; and transforming the way health care providers, police, judges, employers, and others address violence.

Institute on Domestic Violence in the African-American Community
University of Minnesota/School of Social Work
290 Peters Hall
1404 Gortner Avenue
St. Paul, MN 55108-6142
Phone: 877-643-8222
www.dvinstitute.org

The Institute on Domestic Violence in the African-American Community seeks to create a community of African-American scholars and practitioners working in the area of violence in the African-American community, further scholarship in the area of African-American violence, raise community awareness of the impact of violence in the African-American community, inform public policy, organize and facilitate local and national conferences and training forums, and identify community needs and recommend best practices.

Minnesota Center Against Violence and Abuse
School of Social Work
University of Minnesota
105 Peters Hall
1404 Gortner Avenue
St. Paul, MN 55108-6142
Phone: 612-624-0721
www.mincava.umn.edu

The Minnesota Center Against Violence and Abuse (MINCAVA) is an electronic clearinghouse with educational resources about all types of violence, including higher education syllabi, published research, funding sources, upcoming training events, individuals or organizations that serve as resources, and searchable databases with more than seven hundred training manuals, videos, and other education resources. MINCAVA is also part of a cooperative project—Violence Against Women Online Resources—between the center and the U.S. Department of Justice, Office of Justice Programs, Violence Against Women Office. The project's website provides law, criminal justice, and social service professionals with current information about interventions to stop violence against women.

NATIONAL CENTER FOR VICTIMS OF CRIME
2000 M Street NW, Suite 480
Washington, DC 20036
Phone: 202-467-8700
www.ncvc.org

The National Center for Victims of Crime (NCVC) is a nonprofit organization that serves victims of all types of crime, including intimate-partner violence. The center provides public policy advocacy; training and technical assistance to victim service organizations, counselors, attorneys, criminal justice agencies, and allied professionals; a toll-free hotline for crime victims; and a virtual library containing publications, current statistics with references, a list of recommended readings, and bibliographies.

NATIONAL CENTER ON DOMESTIC AND SEXUAL VIOLENCE
7800 Shoal Creek Boulevard, Suite 120-N
Austin, TX 78757
Phone: 512-407-9020
www.ncdsv.org

The National Center on Domestic and Sexual Violence develops and provides innovative training and consultation, influences policy, and promotes collaboration and diversity in working to end domestic and sexual violence. NCDSV has a staff of nationally known trainers and sponsors national and regional conferences.

NATIONAL COALITION AGAINST DOMESTIC VIOLENCE
P.O. Box 18749
Denver, CO 80218
Phone: 303-839-1852
www.ncadv.org

The National Coalition Against Domestic Violence (NCADV) is a membership organization of domestic violence coalitions and service programs. NCADV provides training, technical assistance, legislative and policy advocacy, and promotional and educational materials and products on domestic violence; coordinates a national collaborative effort to assist battered women in removing the physical scars of abuse; and works to raise awareness about domestic violence.

NATIONAL DOMESTIC VIOLENCE HOTLINE
P.O. Box 161810
Austin, TX 78716
Hotline: 800-779-SAFE (7233)
TTY: 800-787-3224
Administrative phone: 512-453-8117
www.ndvh.org

The National Domestic Violence Hotline connects individuals to help in their area using a nationwide database that includes detailed information about domestic violence shelters, other emergency shelters, legal advocacy and assistance programs, and social service programs. Help is available in English or Spanish, twenty-four hours a day, seven days a week. Interpreters are available to translate an additional 139 languages.

NATIONAL LATINO ALLIANCE FOR THE
ELIMINATION OF DOMESTIC VIOLENCE
P.O. Box 322086
Fort Washington Station
New York, NY 10032
Phone: 646-672-1404 or 800-342-9908
www.DVAlianza.org

The National Latino Alliance for the Elimination of Domestic Violence (the Alianza) is a group of nationally recognized Latina and Latino advocates, community activists, practitioners, researchers, and survivors of domestic violence working together to promote understanding, sustain dialogue, and generate solutions to end domestic violence affecting Latino communities, with an understanding of the sacredness of all relationships and communities. Support from the Administration on Children and Families, Department of Health and Human Services, has allowed the Alianza to establish El Centro: National Latino Research Center on Domestic Violence and the Alianza Training and Technical Assistance Division.

National Native American Resources to End Violence Against Native Women

P.O. Box 638
Kyle, SD 57752
Phone: 877-733-7623 (RED-ROAD)

The resource center provides technical assistance, policy development, training institutes, and resource information regarding domestic violence and sexual assault to develop coordinated agency responses in American Indian/Alaska Native tribal communities.

National Network on Behalf of Battered Immigrant Women

www.endabuse.org/programs

The National Network on Behalf of Battered Immigrant Women was cofounded in 1994 by the Family Violence Prevention Fund, AYUDA, NOW Legal Defense and Education Fund, and the National Immigration Project of the National Lawyers Guild to coordinate national advocacy efforts aimed at removing the barriers battered immigrant women and children face when they attempt to leave abusive relationships. Each organization provides leadership in its area of expertise.

National Network to End Domestic Violence

660 Pennsylvania Avenue SE, Suite 303
Washington, DC 20003
Phone: 202-543-5566
www.nnedv.org

The National Network to End Domestic Violence (NNEDV) is a membership and advocacy organization of state domestic violence coalitions. NNEDV provides legislative and policy advocacy on behalf of the state domestic violence coalitions and, through the National Network to End Domestic Violence Fund, provides training, technical assistance, and funds to domestic violence advocates.

National Sexual Violence Resource Center

123 North Enola Drive
Enola, PA 17025
Phone: 717-909-0710
Toll-free: 877-739-3895
www.nsvrc.org

The National Sexual Violence Resource Center (NSVRC) identifies and disseminates information, resources, and research on all aspects of sexual violence prevention and intervention. The NSVRC website features links to related resources and information about conferences, funding, job announcements, and special events. Additional activities include coordinating national sexual assault awareness activities, identifying emerging policy issues and research needs, issuing a biannual newsletter, and recommending speakers and trainers.

National Violence Against Women Prevention Research Center

Phone: 843-792-2945
www.musc.edu/vawprevention

The National Violence Against Women Prevention Research Center provides information that is useful to scientists, practitioners, advocates, grassroots organizations, and any other professional or lay person interested in current topics related to violence against women and its prevention.

National Women's Health Information Center

Office on Women's Health
Department of Health and Human Services
200 Independence Avenue SW, Room 730B
Washington, DC 20201

Phone: 202-690-7650
www.womenshealth.gov

The National Women's Health Information Center (NWHIC), run by the Office on Women's Health, is the most current and reliable resource on women's health today. It provides links to a wide range of women's health–related material developed by the Department of Health and Human Services, other federal agencies, and private sector resources.

Rape, Abuse & Incest National Network (RAINN)

Hotline: 800-656-HOPE (4673)
www.rainn.org

The Rape, Abuse & Incest National Network (RAINN) is the nation's largest anti–sexual-assault organization. RAINN's national hotline works as a call-routing system. When an individual calls RAINN, a computer reads the area code and first three digits of the phone number and routes the call to the nearest member rape crisis center.

The Stalking Resource Center

National Center for Victims of Crime
2000 M Street NW, Suite 480
Washington, DC 20036
Phone: 202-467-8700
Fax: 202-467-8701
www.ncvc.org/src/main.aspx

The Stalking Resource Center is a project of the National Center for Victims of Crime, funded through the Violence Against Women Office (VAWO), U.S. Department of Justice. The Stalking Resource Center has established a clearinghouse of information and resources to inform and support local, multidisciplinary stalking-response programs nationwide; developed a national peer-to-peer exchange program to provide targeted, on-site problem-solving assistance to VAWO Arrest grantee jurisdictions; and organized a nationwide network of local practitioners representing VAWO grantee jurisdictions to support their multidisciplinary approaches to stalking.

U.S. Department of Justice

Office for Victims of Crime Resource Center
National Criminal Justice Reference Service
P.O. Box 6000
Rockville, MD 20849-6000
Phone: 800-627-6872
TTY: 877-712-9279
www.ojp.usdoj.gov/ovc/

The Office for Victims of Crime (OVC) was established by the 1984 Victims of Crime Act to oversee diverse programs that benefit victims of crime. OVC provides substantial funding to state victim assistance and compensation programs—the lifeline services that help victims to heal. The agency supports trainings designed to educate criminal justice and allied professionals about the rights and needs of crime victims. OVC also sponsors an annual event in April to commemorate National Crime Victims Rights Week.

U.S. Department of Justice

Violence Against Women Office
810 7th Street NW
Washington, DC 20531
Phone: 202-307-6026
TTY: 202-307-2277
www.ojp.usdoj.gov/vawo/

The Violence Against Women Office works with victim advocates and law enforcement to develop grant programs that support a wide range of services for victims of domestic violence, sexual assault, and stalking, including advocacy, emergency shelter, law enforcement protection, and legal aid. Additionally, the Violence Against Women Office is leading efforts nationally and abroad to intervene in and prosecute crimes of trafficking in women and children and is addressing international domestic violence issues.

Violence Against Women Electronic Network

www.vawnet.org

The National Online Resource Center on Violence Against Women (VAWnet) provides a collection of full-text, searchable resources on domestic violence, sexual violence, and related issues as well as links to an "In the News" section, calendars listing trainings, conferences, grants, and access to the Domestic Violence Awareness Month and Sexual Assault Awareness Month subsites.

Disclaimer

Links to these organizations, which are provided by the Centers for Disease Control and Prevention (CDC), are provided solely as a service. Links do not constitute an endorsement of these organizations or their programs by the authors, the publisher, or the CDC.

Sources

PROLOGUE

"Homicide trends in the U.S./Intimate homicide," U.S. Department of Justice, Bureau of Justice Statistics. September 2004.

"Many Women at Risk of Being Murdered Don't Know It," *Reuters,* October 2003.

1 WHY MARRY?

New Advent/History of Marriage

The Catholic Encyclopedia, volume IX, 1910, Robert Appleton Company, online edition, 2003, K. Knight, updated 18 August 2004.

"Chivalry and Courtly Love," The School for New Learning, DePaul University, Chicago, David L. Simpson, 1998.

"History of Marriage," Sheri and Bob Stritof, About.com.

"History of Marriage," politicalguru-ga, November 9, 2004.

"A Brief History of Marriage," Cindy Kuzma, October 11, 2004. Planned Parenthood Federation of America, Inc.

"The History of Marriage," PageWise, Inc., 2002.

"Early History of Marriage and Women," Lori Anderson, www.cyberparent.com.

Marriage, A History, Stephanie Coontz, Viking, 2005.

The Psychology of Love and Attachment

"The Romantic Love Test: How do we know if we are in Love?" www.tc.umn.edu.

"Love," *Psychology Today,* March/April 1993.

"Sexuality and Love: A Guide to Psychology and Its Practice," www.guidetopsychology.com/sex_love.htm.

"Romantic Love and Attachment Styles—biological behavior systems," About.com.

"Psychological Theories about Dynamics of Love," About.com.

Soul Mate

"To Meet Your Soul Mate, You Must Meet Your Soul," Efraim Eisen, M.F.C.T., and Rosalie Eisen, M.Ed., Jewish Lights Publishing, 2002.

"Soul Mates," About.com.

"Soul Mate Truths and Tips to Make the Most of Your Love Life," About.com.

"Your Soul Mate–Lover in the Wings, or Exquisite Mirage?" Ana Arias Terry, *Conscious Choice,* February 1999.

"Soul Mates," *Psychology Today,* Mar./Apr. 1994.

The Secret Life of the Unborn Child, Tomas Verny, M.D., with John Kelly, Dell Publishing, 1981.

Fairy Tales and Romantic Fantasy

"Mythology Lives! Ancient Stories and Modern Literature," Guidance Associates—videos and DVDs, www.guidanceassociates.com/mythologylives.html.

"The Princess Syndrome," The Age Company, Ltd., August 2004.

"Fairy Tale Romance—What's the Appeal?" *Romantic Times* magazine.

Feminism and Fairy Tales, Karen E. Rowe, Broadview Press, 2002.

"Beware Romantic Fantasy," *The New Intimacy: Discovering the Magic at the Heart of Your Differences,* Judith Sherven and Jim Sniechowski, Toxic Communication, Inc., 1997.

"Debunk Love Myths," ezinearticles.com, August 2004.

"Romantic Jealousy," *Psychology Today,* March 1992.

"Finding Real Love," *Psychology Today,* Jan./Feb. 2001.

Evolutionary Perspective

"Love, Sex & Natural Selection," *The Moral Animal: Evolutionary and Everyday Life,* Robert Wright, Pantheon, 1994.

The History of Human Marriage. Volume: 1, Edward Westermarck, Macmillan, 1921.

"The Potential Relevance of Biology to Social Inquiry," www.questia.com.

"The Evolutionary Perspective of Women, Sex, and Monogamy: Setting the Record Straight," *Evolution's Voyage,* 1996–2004.

2 The Betrayal/Abandonment Killer

"Suburban Madness," *Texas Monthly,* November 2002.

"I could kill him, Harris told teen," *Houston Chronicle,* January 17, 2003.

"Jurors ponder fate of Clara Harris," CNN.com, February 13, 2003.

"Jury slaps Harris with 20 years," *Houston Chronicle,* February 15, 2003.

"Clara Harris: The Woman Who Ran Over Her Cheating Husband," *The Oprah Winfrey Show,* April 23, 2005.

"Betty Broderick: Divorce, Desperation, Death," Court TV, Crime Library.

"Broderick found guilty of killing ex-husband, wife," *Los Angeles Times,* December 11, 1991.

"Broderick gets 32 years to life," *Los Angeles Times,* February 8, 1992.

"Broderick has no regrets in slayings," *Los Angeles Times,* February 11, 1992.

"Betty Broderick," *The Oprah Winfrey Show,* March 2, 1992.

Crimes of Passion, Howard Engel, Key Porter Books, 2001.

Addiction to Love, Susan Peabody, Celestial Arts Printing, 1994.

"The Straight Dope: Do Dentists Have the Highest Suicide Rate?" Chicago Reader Online Rate Sheet, 2001.

The Dangerous Passion, David M. Buss, The Free Press, 2000.

"The Evolution of Jealousy: Did Men and Women, Facing Different Selective Pressures, Evolve Different 'Brand' of Jealousy? Recent Evidence Suggests Not," *American Scientist,* Jan./Feb. 2004.

"Borderline Personality Disorder: Raising Questions, Finding Answers," National Institute of Mental Health, 2001.

The Dark Side of Close Relationships, edited by Brian H. Spitzberg, William R. Cupach, Lawrence Erlbaum Associates, 1998.

Breaking Hearts, Roy F. Baumeister and Sara R. Wotman, Guilford Press, 1992.

Why We Love: The Nature of Chemistry and Romantic Love, Helen Fisher, Henry Holt and Company, 2004.

When She Was Bad, Patricia Pearson, Viking, 1997.

3 THE CONTROL KILLER

The Surgeon's Wife, Keiran Crowley, St. Martin, 2001.

"Police charge a surgeon murdered wife in '85," *The New York Times,* December 9, 1999.

"In trial without a body, prosecutors put a theory on video," *The New York Times,* October 17, 2000.

"Surgeon convicted of murdering wife," *The New York Times,* October 25, 2000.

"Doctor gets 20 years to life for the murder of his wife," *The New York Times,* November 30, 2000.

"Dermatologist faces arraignment today in wife's fatal shooting," *The Boston Globe,* July 18, 2000.

"Sharpe behavior fits pattern in insanity cases but defense strategy remains under wraps," *The Boston Globe,* November 9, 2001.

"Sharpe's wife reared for life affidavit cites 'unstable' nature," *The Boston Globe,* November 9, 2000.

"Doctor details Sharpe's 'disintegration,' says killer unable to stop himself," *The Boston Globe,* November 20, 2001.

"Tacoma police chief dies after shooting wife, self," *The Seattle Times,* April 27, 2003.

"Records reveal Brame failed 1981 mental exam," *The Seattle Times,* May 1, 2004.

"Portrait of a marriage: Crystal Brame feared her angry, controlling husband," *The Seattle Times,* May 4, 2003.

"Official blocked release of rape complaint against Brame," *The Seattle Times,* May 8, 2003.

"Brame's psychological profile reveals reservations, warnings," *The Seattle Times,* May 10, 2003.

"Crystal Brame told assistant chief of threats, notes show," *The Seattle Times,* June 28, 2003.

Intimate Violence, Joseph Scalia, Columbia University Press, 2002.

"When Women Find Love Is Fatal," *The New York Times,* February 15, 2002.

"Dynamics of Partner Violence and Types of Abuse and Abusers," Glenda Kaufman Kantor and Jana L. Jasinski, Family Research Laboratory, University of New Hampshire, 1998.

"Predictors of Domestic Violence Homicide of Women," *American Journal of Public Health,* July 2003.

Dangerous Relationships, Noelle Nelson, Insight Books, 1997.

"The Broken Mirror: A Self Psychological Treatment Perspective for Relationship Violence," David B. Wexler, American Psychiatric Association, April 1999.

Criminal Profiling, Brent Turvey, Academic Press, 2002.

"Losing Control," Holly Johnson and Tina Hotton, *Homicide Studies,* vol. 7, no. 1, February 2003, Sage Publications.

"Homicide Followed by Suicide," *Centre for Suicide Prevention SIEC Alert* is a publication of the Centre for Suicide Prevention.

"Murder Followed by Suicide in Australia, 1973–1992: a research note," Jo Barnes, *Journal of Sociology,* 2002.

"Separation, Divorce and Violence Against Women by Male Partners: Some Canadian examples," Aysan Sev'er, University of Toronto at Scarborough, March 2002.

"The Broken Mirror: A Self Psychological Treatment Perspective for Relationship Violence," David B. Wexler, Ph.D., *Journal of Psychotherapy Practice,* April 1999.

4 THE SOCIOPATHIC KILLER

"The Longo killings: A trail of crimes," *The Oregonian,* January 12, 2002.

"Psychologists say Longo fits chilling profile," *The Oregonian,* January 18, 2002.

"Tourists recall Longo's boasts, carefree ways," *The Oregonian,* January 23, 2002.

"Charmer becomes Murder Defendant," *Detroit Free Press,* January 26, 2002.

"Court documents in Longo case detail killings, disposal of bodies," *The Oregonian,* March 23, 2002.

"Longo recalls his family's final days in interview," *The Oregonian,* December 3, 2002.

"Officials: Ex-Iowan killed family for wild lifestyle," *Daily Iowan,* March 12, 2003.

"Longo says that pride kept him from asking for financial help," *The Oregonian,* March 27, 2003.

"Longo jury will begin deliberations Monday," *The Oregonian,* April 4, 2003.

"Longo defense draws doubts," *The Oregonian,* April 6, 2003.

"Victim's sister helps state wrap up its case seeking death for Longo," *The Oregonian,* April 11, 2003.

"Longo condemned to die," *The Oregonian,* April 17, 2003.

"Prosecutors: Mark shot her," *Salt Lake Tribune,* August 10, 2004.

"Marriage a façade, but Lori was saint," *Deseret Morning News,* October 3, 2004.

"I intentionally shot Lori Hacking," *Salt Lake Tribune,* April 16, 2005.

"The Hour of His Reckoning," *People,* April 18, 2005.

"Tearful ending—Mark Hacking gets 6-life prison term," *Deseret Morning News,* June 7, 2005.

"Psychopathology and Antisocial Personality Disorder: A Journey Into the Abyss," from www.omicidiseriali.it/disorder.htm.

"Antisocial Personality, Sociopathy and Psychopathy," from http://faulty.ncwc.edu/toconnor/428/4281ect16.htm.

The Fifty Minute Hour, Robert Lindner, Other Press, 2002.

Without Conscience, Robert D. Hare, Ph.D., Guilford Press, 1999.

"Romeo's Bleeding When Mr. Right Turns Out to Be Mr. Wrong," OBGYN.net, 1996–2005.

"Domestic Aggression and Traumatic Brain Injury," Deborah Bryon, M.A., LPC, 4therapy.com network, inc., 2004.

"Motives, Malignant Needs, a Father's Entitlement," *Court TV,* Crime Library.

"The Profile: Feelings and Relationships," *Frontline:* the Execution, 1995–2000, WGBH Educational Foundation.

5 THE BLACK WIDOW/PROFIT KILLER

"Georgia woman faces life in prison after two men die of antifreeze poisoning," Court TV.

"Expert: Second dose of poison killed firefighter," Court TV, May 13, 2004.

"Wife found guilty of killing husband with antifreeze," Court TV, May 14, 2004.

"Woman who killed husband with antifreeze indicted for boyfriend's death," The Associated Press, October 5, 2004.

"Prosector: Woman in troubled marriage wanted husband dead," The Associated Press, January 13, 1999.

"Hricko friend describes plan," *The Washington Times,* January 15, 1999.

"Woman convicted of killing husband during Valentine's weekend," CNN.com, January 16, 1999.

"Woman sentenced to life in prison in husband's Valentine's murder," The Associated Press, March 19, 1999.

"Kimberly Michelle Hricko v. *State of Maryland,"* Court of Special Appeals of Maryland, September 1999.

Female Crime and Delinquency, Coramae Richey Mann, University of Alabama Press, 1984.

"Violence in Dulcet Tones," Court TV, Crime Library.

"Domestic Homicide of Male Spouses by Females," Lt. Cynthia T. Ferguson, CNM, MSN, Forensic Nurse, Virgo Publishing, Inc., 2004.

"The Story of Valentine's Day," www.holidays.net/amore/story.html.

Murder Most Rare: The Female Serial Killer, Michael D. Kelleher and C. L. Kelleher, Dell, 1999.

When She Was Bad: Violent Women and the Myth of Innocence, Patricia Pearson, Viking, 1997.

6 THE NARCISSISTIC KILLER

"Rabbi's ex-lover recounts affair," *Philadelphia Daily News,* October 23, 2002.

"2 testify rabbi wanted wife dead," *Philadelphia Daily News,* October 24, 2002.

"Hit man retells slaying of rabbi's wife," *Philadelphia Daily News,* November 2, 2002.

"Jury finds rabbi guilty in murder plot," *The New York Times,* November 21, 2002.

"Rabbi convicted of killing wife gets life sentence," *Philadelphia Inquirer,* January 17, 2003.

"Sins of the Rabbi," *ABC News 20/20,* April 11, 2003.

"Investigative report: Why husbands kill their wives," *The Oprah Winfrey Show,* April 1, 2004.

"3 guilty in N.H. Killing, agree to testify in widow's trial," *The Boston Globe,* January 30, 1991.

"Smart is found guilty," *The Boston Globe,* March 23, 1991.

"Pam Smart's lover, accomplice in murder, sentenced to 28 years," The Associated Press, August 19, 1992.

"Did she love Billy Flynn? Pam Smart tells TV show," *The Union Leader,* January 19, 1995.

"Pamela Smart: An Interview with a life prisoner," *ABC News Primetime Live,* July 12, 1995.

Malignant Self Love—Narcissism Revisited, Sam Vaknin, Narcissus Publication, 2005.

Essential Papers on Narcissism, edited by Andrew P. Morrison, M.Dm, New York University Press, 1986.

Horoscope Analysis, ivillage.com, 2005.

7 The Temper Tantrum Killer

"Peterson found guilty of killing pregnant wife," *Los Angeles Times,* November 13, 2004.

"The Peterson case," *San Francisco Chronicle,* March 18, 2005.

"The Laci Peterson Case," Courttv.com.

"Cased closed," Cumberlink.com, January 1, 2005.

"Is Warwick grad a hit man?" *Lancaster New Era,* October 1, 2003.

"Ex-Lititz resident convicted in murder scheme," *Lancaster New Era,* April 20, 2004.

"Ex-county man gets life for murder for hire," *Lancaster Intelligencer Journal,* May 7, 2004.

The New Psychoanalysis, Phyllis W. Meadow, Rowman & Littlefield Publishers, Inc., 2003.

Intimate Violence, Joseph Scalia, Columbia University Press, 2002.

"What is Multiple Sclerosis?" National Multiple Sclerosis Society, July 2004.

"Teaching Your Child Self-Control," *KidsHealth,* The Nemours Foundations, 1995–2005.

"The Truth About Temper Tantrums," *KidsHealth,* The Nemours Foundations, 1995–2005.

8 THE TRANSFERENCE KILLER

"The Staircase & The Novelist's Wife," Courttv.com.
"1985 death continues to dominate novelist's murder trial," Courttv.com, August 26, 2003.
"Closing arguments set in novelist trial," Courttv.com, September 30, 2003.
"Betrayed by Her Own Children," *CBS News,* August 4, 2004.
"For Love or Money," *CBS News,* August 4, 2004.
"A Family Friend Questioned," *CBS News,* August 4, 2004.
"Beards were loving couple, friend testifies," *The Austin American Statesman,* March 7, 2003.
"Texas, Money & Murder," *ABC Primetime Live,* April 10, 2003.
"Living Large," *CBS News 48 Hours Investigates,* May 14, 2003.
"Marriage, Money and Murder," *People,* August 11, 2003.
"Friends or Lovers?" *CBS News,* August 4, 2004.
"Who Will the Jury Believe?" *CBS News,* August 4, 2004.
Attachment Disorder Experts: Psychological Services for Reactive Attachment Disorder, Evergreen Psychotherapy Center Attachment Treatment & Training Institute, 2004.
"Perspectives on intimate partner murders," P. Mercader, A. Houel, H. Sobota, 2003.
"Intimate Partner Violence: PTSD, Combat, & Abuse History," *The Repetition & Avoidance Quarterly,* The Washington Veterans PTSD Program, 2003.
She Wanted It All, Kathryn Casey, Avon Books, 2005.
When She Was Bad, Patricia Pearson, Viking, 1997.
"Thoughts on Contemporary Psychoanalytic Theory," Joyce Edward, CSW, BCD, www.psycjourney.com, 2004.
"Types of Psychological Treatment," *A Guide to Psychology and Its Practice,* 1997–2005.
"Male Perpetrators of Violence Against Women: An Attachment Theory Perspective," Peter Fonagy, Ph.D., *Psych Matters,* 2004.
"The Neurobiology of Abandonment Homicide," Donald G. Dutton, *Aggression and Violent Behavior,* 7, 1–5, 2001.

"To Have and to Kill," by Stephen G. Michaud. www.stephenmichaud.com, 1999.

9 The Revenge Killer

"Woman charged with murder for stabbing husband 193 times," *Houston Chronicle,* January 24, 2003.

"*Texas* v. *Wright:* Wife stabs husband to death," Court TV.

"Prosecutors show version of Wright attack," *Houston Chronicle,* February 26, 2004.

"Wright jury hears 2 sides of 'terror,' " *Houston Chronicle,* February 26, 2004.

"Graphic autopsy photos shown in Susan Wright murder trial," *KRTK,* February 26, 2004.

"Murder or Self-Defense?" The Associated Press, March 3, 2004.

"Night of Terror: Susan Wright's account of the night she killed her husband," *CBS News/48 Hours,* April 24, 2004.

"Family Portrait: Relationship of Jeff and Susan Wright," *CBS News/48 Hours,* July 21, 2004.

"Final Secret: Allegations that Susan Wright's own mother was abused by her father," *CBS News/48 Hours,* July 21, 2004.

"Slaying shatters image of perfect life," *Detroit Free Press,* May 14, 2004.

"Cops: Tempers flared, wife killed husband with ax," *Detroit Free Press,* May 15, 2004.

"Farmington Hills teacher charged in stabbing death of husband," The Associated Press, May 15, 2004.

"Mom on trial was the victim, son insists," *Detroit Free Press,* November 27, 2004.

"Ex-teacher's trial begins," *The Detroit News,* December 1, 2004.

"Son says father abused mother," *The Daily Oakland Press,* December 4, 2004.

"Wife accused of murdering husband testifies to abuse," *The Daily Oakland Press,* December 7, 2004.

"Seaman recounts axing her husband," *The Detroit News,* December 8, 2004.

"Wife guilty of killing husband," *The Daily Oakland Press,* December 16, 2004.

Why We Hate, Rush W. Dozier, Jr., Contemporary Books, 2002.
"War Crimes of the Heart," *Psychology Today,* September 1992.
"Anger," Raymond Lloyd Richmond, Ph.D., A Guide to Psychology and Its Practice. www.guidetopsychology.com, 2005.
"Desperation feeds on anger, isolation," *The Chicago Tribune,* March 11, 2005.
"Celebrating Mother's Day," www.holidays.net/mother/celebrat.2005.
"Revenge Is Indeed Sweet, Study Finds," The Associated Press, August 26, 2004.
When She Was Bad, Patricia Pearson, Viking, 1997.
"Battered Wives, Battered Justice," *National Review,* February 25, 1991.
"Battered Wife Syndrome Defense a First in RP courts," Inquirer News Service, January 25, 2004.

10 THE PREGNANCY KILLER

"Murder trial of former NFL star Rae Carruth," *CNBC Dan Abrams,* December 21, 2000.
"Murder: The Leading Cause of Death for Pregnant Women," The Associated Press, April 23, 2003.
"Many New or Expectant Mothers Die Violent Deaths," *The Washington Post,* December 18, 2004.
"Report: Carruth paid to have girlfriend beaten," *The Detroit News,* March 30, 2000.
"Carruth playing for his life," Courttv.com.
"Ex-flame testifies Carruth confessed to her," Court TV.
"Carruth gets stiff sentence," Courttv.com.
"Presumed Innocent," *Time,* January 22, 1990.
"The Forgotten Victim: The Collision of Race, Gender, and Murder—Was It Worth It?" February 1990.
"Dynamics of Partner Violence and Types of Abuse and Abusers," Glenda Kaufman Kantor and Jana L. Jasinki, Family Research Laboratory, University of New Hampshire.
"The Hidden Suffering of the Psychopath," Willem H. J. Martens, M.D., Ph.D., *Psychiatric Times,* January 2002.
Intimate Violence, Joseph Scalia, Columbia University Press, 2002.
Happy Though Pregnant, Hyman Spotnitz and Lucy Freeman, Berkley Publishing Corporation, 1969.

"Intimate Partner Homicide," NewsFlash, an online newsletter of the Family Violence Prevention Fund.

"Motherhood Cut Short: When Pregnancy Ends in Murder," Court TV, September 3, 2004.

"Many New or Expectant Mothers Die Violent Deaths," Donna St. George, American College of Nurse-Midwives, December 19, 2004.

11 THE CAREGIVER KILLER

Roswell Gilbert, *Appellant* v. *State of Florida,* Appellee, 559 So. 2d 225; 1990 Fla. App.

Marriage in Motion, Richard Schwartz, M.D., and Jacqueline Olds, M.D., Perseus Publishing, 2002.

"Homicide-Suicide in Older Persons," Donna Cohen, Ph.D., Maria Llorente, M.D., and Carl Eisdorfer, Ph.D., M.D., *Am. J. Psychiatry,* March 1998.

"Violence in home is unwanted guest," Denise Nelesen, Signonsandiego.com, August 2003.

"Domestic Abuse Later in Life," VAWnet, 2003.

Index